S0-GGP-433

METROPOLITAN ACTION STUDIES NO. 4

Growth

and Government

in Sacramento

THE AUTHORS

JAMES R. BELL, Professor of Government and Coordinator of Public Administration Curricula, Sacramento State College

LEONARD D. CAIN, JR., Professor and Head, Department of Sociology, Sacramento State College

LYMAN A. GLENNY, Executive Director, Board of Higher Education, State of Illinois

WILLIAM H. HICKMAN, Professor and Head, Department of Economics, Sacramento State College

IRL A. IRWIN, Associate Professor of Psychology, Sacramento State College

CHRISTIAN L. LARSEN, Professor and Head, Department of Government and Police Science, Sacramento State College

METROPOLITAN ACTION STUDIES NO. 4

Growth and Government in Sacramento

CHRISTIAN L. LARSEN

JAMES R. BELL

LEONARD D. CAIN, JR.

LYMAN A. GLENNY

WILLIAM H. HICKMAN

IRL A. IRWIN

BLOOMINGTON · INDIANA UNIVERSITY PRESS · LONDON

ALL RIGHTS RESERVED

Copyright © 1965 by Indiana University Press
Manufactured in the United States of America
Library of Congress catalog card number: 65-19708

JS
1372
S32
L3

Contents

1 1 1 3 3 8

Tables, Maps

Foreword

The most difficult and complex problems of domestic public policy of our time and nation are associated with the changing characteristics of the urban community. Congestion, deterioration, and delinquency in the older cities; ugliness and sprawl in the suburbs; the tensions accompanying social and economic segregation as the exploding populations group and regroup themselves into communities which only inadequately provide for common purposes and the public welfare—these are pervasive and endemic in current American society.

The institutions and arrangements for confronting the basic public policy questions lag behind the needs of changing social patterns. There is often no appropriate forum, no viable governmental entity, through which community decisions can be considered and reached. Nearly all American cities, faced with institutional inadequacies, have struggled with the need to adjust their govermental units and agencies to cope with the problems of urban services and urban direction.

This is the fourth in a group of case studies of the efforts of particular American cities to adapt and adjust their governmental institutions to the new metropolitan problems. *Decisions in Syracuse* (1961), *The Miami Metropolitan Experiment* (1963), and *The Milwaukee Metropolitan Study Commission* (1965), all published by the Indiana University Press, have preceded it. The four cities described in these case studies differ significantly, yet there is much in common in their problems and in their reactions to the problems. Sacramento, capital city of the state which is now the most populous in the union, is frequently overshadowed in national image by its two giant metropolitan neighbors, Los Angeles and San Francisco, but it is itself clearly representative of the new and rapidly growing cities of the West. Much newer and more dynamic in growth than Syracuse or Milwaukee, it is not yet as large as Miami. Its approaches to the governmental problems of rapid urban expansion are not the same as those in the other three cities, but its use of citizen study committees and of outside consultants, of petitions and referenda, have obvious counterparts in the other cities.

These case studies were supported by a series of grants from the Ford Foundation; a grant was also made to Indiana University to enable it to attempt some coordination of the individual studies. The investigations were conducted, in each instance, by a group of social scientists at a university or college in the metropolitan community involved. The authors of this study were members of the faculty at Sacramento State College.

Through this and the other volumes of the series, we hope that a better understanding of the processes of governmental adaptation to social change, and of community decision-making in general, will be promoted.

Indiana University   YORK WILLBERN

Preface

In 1959 the Sacramento State College Foundation received a
grant from the Ford Foundation to study the governmental reorganization attempts of the Sacramento metropolitan area.
The study was proposed and executed by three political scientists, one economist, one sociologist, and one psychologist—all
from the Sacramento State College faculty. Professor Larsen, a
political scientist, was designated by the group to direct the
study.

The grant for this study was one of several made for the
study of particular communities and their efforts toward solving specific metropolitan area problems. The studies are in-
tended to serve both comparative and historical purposes. The
specific purpose of the grant was to "capture and record"
experiences of metropolitan areas. The study was also to be
interdisciplinary and to be completed within a two-year period.

The goals and research methods of the Sacramento study
were, of course, affected by the terms and purposes of the
grant.[1] To have examined in detail all aspects of the governmental units, the personal attributes of public officeholders,

the total pattern of interest groupings, and all other possible
influences on the reorganization movements not only would
have been beyond the resources of time and money available
to the research committee, but could well have buried the
significance of the primary purpose of "capturing and record-
ing." The committee had to decide which areas to study in
order to "capture" the salient influences in the reorganization
attempts. Three different classifications of groups could be
identified in these attempts: the special interest groups such
as realtors, merchants, suburban newspapers, school officials,
and local government officials and employees; the civic organizations interested in good government such as the League of
Women Voters, neighborhood improvement clubs, and various
study committees; and the people active in the movements
themselves. In the final analysis, we abandoned depth studies
of groups and sample polls of residents in favor of presenting
the third group—the people who were active in the reorganization movements—in sharp focus. The group also decided that,
in order to present a meaningful picture of attempted governmental changes, the description of events ought to be aug-
mented by a study of the leadership power structure in the
area. The following statement served as a guide throughout
the study:

> To capture and record the history of efforts since the mid-
> 1940's to secure modification of the governmental forms
> serving the Sacramento metropolitan area. To attempt to
> identify, describe, and analyze the forces, opinions, atti-
> tudes, obstacles, and associated factors at work in the
> community relative to the changes which have occurred
> and the changes which have been proposed as to local
> governmental arrangements. To describe and evaluate the
> effectiveness of community-wide leadership and organiza-
> tion as they apply to the metropolitan area.

The major source of information for these reorganization
movements was extensive personal interviews with a total of

96 residents of the Sacramento area. These persons were selected because of their activity in one or more specific movements for change or because they were generally acknowledged to be influential in the metropolitan area as a whole. The authors also relied upon newspaper accounts and official documents of groups involved in the reorganization attempts (see Appendix).

Some economic, political, and social background is included when necessary to clarify an action or attitude, but the main emphasis is on description and analysis of the action groups connected with reorganization efforts. Interest groups and "good government" organizations were not studied directly, but were evaluated by the activists in the movements, in interviews and questionnaires. Persons who had not participated in reorganization attempts but who held power and influence in the community were also studied. The reorganization efforts are presented in chronological order and in some sense re-enact the give-and-take between the participants in the movements. The interpretations and evaluations of the authors are, for the most part, postponed until the concluding chapters.

The study committee has not recommended an appropriate governmental structure for the metropolitan area; this was not the purpose of the grant. Observations and suggestions from persons who were interviewed are included, but no single comprehensive solution is suggested and no solution mentioned is endorsed by the study group.

The authors are most grateful to the following organizations and individuals: the Ford Foundation for the generous grant which made this study possible; all the interviewees, who so graciously gave us time from busy schedules and whose contributions to the study cannot be overrated; Mrs. Doris Hollister, Dr. James Cowan, Mr. Walter Isenberg, and Dr. Hubert J. McCormick, for allowing the use of the official minutes and the newspaper histories of the organizations with which they were associated; graduate assistants Thomas Cuny, John Lopes, and Robert Curry, who did an excellent job of locating and organizing materials; Michael Cullivan and John Berg for excellent services in preparing the maps; Miss Nancy Ryan and Miss Nina McCoy for providing capable typing and stenographic assistance, often under the most trying conditions; and Dr. Ernest G. Miller, whose editorial services gave added emphasis to the central theme of this study.

CHRONOLOGICAL OUTLINE OF GOVERNMENTAL REORGANIZATION EVENTS

September-October, 1955—Publication of 19 articles in *Sacramento Bee* on "Sacramento's Community Crisis."

November, 1955—Sacramento Metropolitan Area Advisory Committee (SMAAC) authorized.

February 1, 1956—First meeting of SMAAC.

May 9, 1956—Public Administration Service employed by SMAAC.

September, 1956—Publication of the report of the Urban Government Committee of the Greater North Area Chamber of Commerce entitled *Problems of Local Government in the Greater North Area of Sacramento County.*

November 13, 1956—PAS issued the first preliminary report.

February 19, 1957—PAS issued the second preliminary report.

May 22, 1957—PAS final report released.

November 12, 1957—SMAAC issued its final report relative to the PAS report.

December 18, 1957—Decision made to terminate SMAAC and to create a new committee—the Metropolitan Government Committee (MGC).

January 13, 1958—Final meeting of SMAAC.

February 19, 1958—First meeting of MGC.

June 17, 1958—Proposal to incorporate a big new city made public.

July 3, 1958—Sacramento City Council approval of the proposal to annex the Hagginwood-Del Paso Heights area requested.

November 18, 1958—Effort to incorporate a big new city abandoned.

December 18, 1958—Sacramento City Council approval of the proposal to annex Arden-Arcade requested.

January 20, 1959—Hagginwood-Del Paso Heights annexation proposal defeated by voters.

March 5, 1959—MGC adopted the proposal of mass annexation plus city-county consolidation of some services.

June, 1959—MGC issued its final report entitled *Government Reorganization for Metropolitan Sacramento.*

September 29, 1959—Proposed Arden-Arcade annexation defeated by voters.

June 2, 1964—Voters of North Sacramento approve merger with Sacramento.

METROPOLITAN ACTION STUDIES NO. 4

Growth

and Government

in Sacramento

1

Metropolitan Sacramento

Sacramento, not only the Valley's chief city, but the even
busier capital of a rich, progressive . . . state, is in the
midst of the most phenomenal expansion of all. It is in
the midst of it, but curiously apart.[1]

Sacramento, the "Camellia Capital of the World," spreads
eastward from the confluence of the Sacramento and American
rivers and dominates the northern part of the 450-mile long
great Central Valley that lies between the Sierra Nevada to the
east and the Coast Range to the west. Sacramento County,
which by U.S. Bureau of the Census definition was also the
Sacramento metropolitan area when this study was undertaken,
has grown to a population of over one-half million people.
Between 1950 and 1960 the population increased by more than
225,000. The communities surrounding the capital city have
grown faster than the city of Sacramento has. Sacramento has
been cited as "a classic example of a small American city that

3

is subject to rather than master of today's powerful new social, economic, and political pressures. . . ."[2] Although the outlying communities have strong ties to the central city, Sacramento, they continue to be governed as small, separate units.

Unless otherwise indicated, in this study Sacramento County is considered as being the Sacramento metropolitan area, since the U.S. Bureau of the Census used this definition of a metropolitan area at the time this study was begun. If any part of a county is considered part of a metropolitan area, then the entire county is so considered. It should be noted, however, that certain areas of neighboring counties are a part of the Sacramento community in a social and an economic sense whereas the southern part of Sacramento County really is not. Certainly, the portion of Yolo County lying just across the Sacramento River to the west of Sacramento city is a part of the Sacramento community. Urban developments along the Roseville freeway have brought the city of Roseville (Placer County) and its surrounding area into the Sacramento metropolitan area in the same sense. This hardly can be said of Isleton, a small incorporated municipality many miles to the south and west of Sacramento city but contained within Sacramento County. An awareness of this difference between the county boundaries and a realistic definition of the metropolitan community was indicated by the Public Administration Service in its survey, *The Government of Metropolitan Sacramento*, published in 1957. However, the Public Administration Service decided not to cross county boundary lines in its study, on the ground that California constitutional complications and political considerations made any approach to metropolitan problems other than one based on the county virtually impossible to put into effect.

During the late 1950's several attempts were made to reorganize the governmental structure of the metropolitan area.

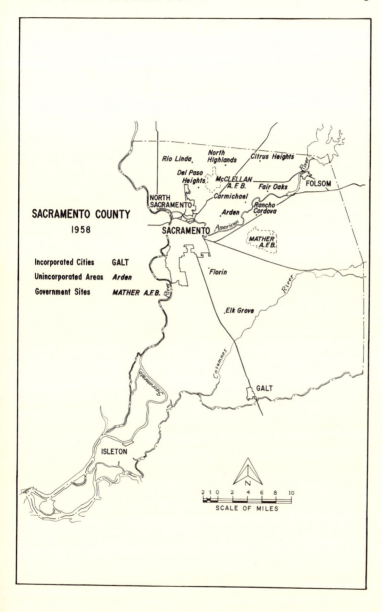

SACRAMENTO COUNTY
1958

Incorporated Cities   **GALT**
Unincorporated Areas   *Arden*
Government Sites   *MATHER A.F.B.*

Rio Linda
North Highlands
Citrus Heights
Del Paso Heights
McCLELLAN A.F.B.
Fair Oaks
FOLSOM
NORTH SACRAMENTO
Carmichael
Rancho Cordova
Arden
SACRAMENTO
American
MATHER A.F.B.
Florin
Elk Grove
GALT
ISLETON

N

2 1 0   2   4   6   8   10
SCALE OF MILES

Two groups were established to study the problem of governing in the entire area. Two large areas outside the city of Sacramento considered and voted on the question of annexation to the city of Sacramento. One area attempted to incorporate itself as one large city, separate from the city of Sacramento. Because of their related, often overlapping nature, these reorganizational attempts may be viewed as parts of a single, wide-ranging response to the problem of governance in the Sacramento metropolitan area. This study is essentially a record of these movements and an analysis of the citizens' response to them.

Since none of these attempts to consolidate governments in the Sacramento area was accepted by the citizenry at the time (the Hagginwood-Del Paso Heights area annexation has been achieved in more recent years), the conclusions about governmental reorganization so far indicate concrete achievements to have been quite limited. An important problem dealt with in this study, however, is why these attempts at change failed. Answers to this question cannot be found without an understanding of the nature of the communities involved and a recognition of the leading individuals and organizations in the area. Through study of the records of the groups involved in the reorganization efforts, through newspaper accounts, and through extensive interviews with community leaders and leaders in the movements, we attempt to paint a broad picture of the arena in which decisions about governance in the Sacramento metropolitan area have been made.

THE SETTING

Sacramento, the capital of California, is the chief city in a large and rich agricultural area located at the confluence of two of the largest rivers in northern California. Its steady and

rather spectacular growth can be attributed largely to the
burgeoning state government and to the expansion of federal
field offices. The city has experienced a stable government
devoted to city interests and committed, at least on the record,
to maintaining a good level of municipal services while holding
down property taxes. The city has been accused of being smug,
parochial, and conservative, and this attitude may be traced in
part to the rural background of the central city. This insular
point of view is countered by the incipient urbanism resulting
primarily from many annexations, which have substantially
increased Sacramento's population and have extended its geographical area. In spite of the fact that the population outside
the city is growing faster, Sacramento remains the largest distinct governmental, business, and residential entity in the
metropolitan area.

The postwar growth of the metropolitan area has increased
the size and strengthened the separate identity of several unincorporated business and residential clusters that have grown
up in Sacramento County. In a sense they have grown separately, and in some respects, competitively. Their facilities for
retail trade and services appeal to the suburbanites. Since the
suburban trend after World War II, many new neighborhood
centers have emerged in the county, which have been groping
for some sense of their identity and seeking an influential role
commensurate with their size and economic importance. Each
of these subcommunities, with its loosely defined and overlapping geographical boundaries, claims a degree of loyalty or
attachment from its residents. For instance, the northeast area
includes Arden, Arcade, Country Club Centre, Town and
Country, North Highlands, Citrus Heights, Orangevale, and
others. These groupings may be further subdivided into loyalty associations of improvement clubs and park or other special districts. Several of these larger neighborhood clusters

exceed in population any of the cities in the county except Sacramento.

While the people in these areas consider themselves an important part of Sacramento County, the interview results in this study show that they do not associate their area with any of the cities or share a general sense of community in any tangible, meaningful form. One of their characteristics is rivalry, among themselves and with the city of Sacramento. These localized loyalties are not sufficiently strong to promote incorporation as separate cities but, at the same time, attachments have been strong enough to prevent annexation or incorporation into larger units.

THE CITY OF SACRAMENTO

The city of Sacramento, the largest and first of the five (now four since the merger of North Sacramento with Sacramento) municipalities to be incorporated (August 1, 1849), was granted a charter by the state legislature on February 27, 1850. Its present charter dates back to June 30, 1921. The original boundaries of the city, which encompassed 4.5 square miles, remained unchanged for 65 years. With the annexation of the Oak Park area southeast of Sacramento in 1911, the city limits were extended by 9.4 square miles. No other territory was annexed until 1946, but from that year to 1955, 27 annexations, totaling approximately 9.5 square miles, took place.

Possibly because of the work of the Sacramento Metropolitan Area Advisory Committee and the Public Administration Service, the nationally known consulting firm employed by the committee, no annexation occurred during 1956 and 1957. Several annexations (and one merger) have taken place since then, adding about 69.29 square miles to the city. As of June, 1965, its total area was approximately 92.75 square miles.

Sacramento's annexations, for the most part, have extended

the city's boundaries eastward to the American River and southward for several miles. The annexation, as uninhabited territory, of the new site for the California State Fair in 1959 represented the first acquisition of territory across the American River. This extended the area of Sacramento city to that side of the American River where most of the people of Sacramento County's unincorporated area live. In early 1961 Sacramento's first inhabited area across the river, Northgate, was annexed, and the additional annexation in May, 1961, of approximately 8.5 square miles of contiguous uninhabited territory opened the gate for further expansion into the North Area.

OTHER INCORPORATED AREAS

The city of Sacramento was the county's only incorporated municipality until 1923, when Isleton, a small city in the delta area of the southwestern portion of the county, was incorporated. The census reports for Isleton show a population decline from 1,837 in 1940 to 1,039 in 1960. The municipality has had three small annexations and has a total area of between one-fourth and one-third of a square mile.

North Sacramento was incorporated in 1924. Annexations to the city of Sacramento had resulted in North Sacramento being completely surrounded by Sacramento by the time merger of the two municipalities was approved by North Sacramento voters in June of 1964. North Sacramento got off to a shaky start, when a petition to disincorporate was circulated during the first year of its existence. Its first annexation, in 1939, plus others in the post World War II period, enlarged North Sacramento's area from .75 to 6.58 square miles by the time of the merger. Its 1960 population of 12,922 represented an increase of about 100 per cent over the 1950 figure.

In April, 1946, Folsom became Sacramento County's fourth incorporated municipality. It is situated on the banks of the

American River, approximately 25 miles to the east and north of the city of Sacramento. Until 1959, when it annexed territory across the American River and up to the Placer County line, Folsom lay entirely on the south side of the river. Folsom has actively annexed in recent years, and by January, 1965, it had an area of approximately 7.5 square miles. Its 1960 population was 3,925, compared with 1,690 in 1950.

In August, 1946, Galt, which is located about 30 miles southeast of the city of Sacramento, became the fifth incorporated municipality in Sacramento County. A few small annexations to Galt have been made, and its total area is approximately 1.35 square miles. Its population has risen somewhat—from 1,333 in 1950 to 1,868 in 1960.

The incorporated cities of Isleton, Folsom, and Galt have their own civic identity and pride, and outwardly, at least, they have few ties with Sacramento or with each other. They are self-reliant, and jealous of their municipal status and prerogatives.

SACRAMENTO COUNTY AND URBANIZED UNINCORPORATED AREAS

Sacramento was far from being a metropolitan area in 1850, when the county was created.[3] The entire population of the county numbered only 9,087. Prior to World War II, Sacramento County was agricultural and rural, typical of counties throughout the country. Mushrooming suburban tracts that have grown up since that time have encircled the incorporated communities and now occupy much of the northern half of the county. The population increased by over 225,000 between 1950 and 1960, and the growth of Sacramento County since the middle 1940's had equaled its growth for all the preceding years (see Table 1). In the 1960 census it ranked eighth among the California counties.[4]

The county has become increasingly urban in function and,

since the mid-1950's, urban in attitude. The area of the county is approximately 983 square miles, and only about 102 of these lay within municipal boundaries as of June, 1965. Although the 1950 census reported more people living within municipalities than outside, by 1960 the proportions had changed— 211,421 of Sacramento County's residents lived in the incorporated municipalities, and 291,357 lived outside. Most of the latter reside in the northern one-third of Sacramento County, bordering upon the city of Sacramento.

A new county manager and a "reformed" board of supervisors have provided the sprawling suburban area with some municipal-type services—generally through a hodgepodge of overlapping special districts. While each district meets a need of some segment of the population, in the aggregate these districts are unplanned and disorderly. According to the Public Administration Service, there were 157 special districts (exclusive of school districts), created under 27 separate laws, as of February, 1957. The few special districts that have been abolished or consolidated since 1957 have been offset by the creation of new districts. Only Los Angeles County exceeds Sacramento in number of special districts.[5]

Compared with many metropolitan areas, Sacramento's governmental pattern might not seem overwhelmingly complicated, nor so difficult to streamline. There are only four incorporated municipalities in the county, containing less than one-ninth of the total county area. The great increase in population has taken place primarily during the past 20 years; the total population of the unincorporated areas has surpassed the total population of the incorporated areas only in the past ten years. The people outside the cities have had little time to develop interests and loyalties that might conflict with efforts at governmental consolidation.

Consolidation or unification has been difficult nevertheless.

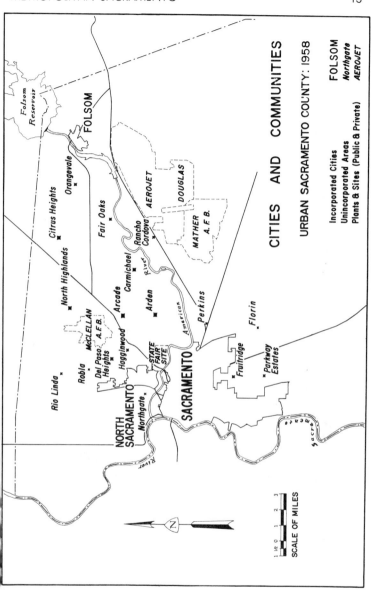

CITIES AND COMMUNITIES

URBAN SACRAMENTO COUNTY: 1958

Incorporated Cities   **FOLSOM**
Unincorporated Areas   *Northgate*
Plants & Sites (Public & Private)   *AEROJET*

SCALE OF MILES

Many distinct but unincorporated communities, once agricultural, have developed, originally around the crossroads store, the rural church, the country school, and the fire station. During the many years that these communities were small in area and population, a strong feeling of separate identity grew up. As they became a part of the urbanized area of metropolitan Sacramento some residents retained this attachment. Among these, Carmichael, Fair Oaks, Orangevale, Citrus Heights, and Florin are all now part of the urban complex extending north and east from the city of Sacramento.

Also, ordinarily urban expansion would take in first those areas adjacent to the central city, since municipal-type services could be extended to such new developments without great difficulty. But the areas adjacent to Sacramento had problems of drainage, seepage, and river overflow. Real estate developers found it more expedient to begin their subdivisions a few miles beyond the boundaries of the city of Sacramento. In addition, the first residential subdivisions were built close to the major suburban employers such as McClellan Air Force Base, Mather Air Force Base, Aerojet-General Corporation, and Douglas Aircraft. The territory between these outlying residential developments and the municipal boundaries of Sacramento gradually became urbanized, but in the meantime a number of the outlying communities such as North Highlands, Rancho Cordova, Parkway Estates, Arden, and Arcade developed a sense of separate identity.

As population increased, the unincorporated areas created special districts to provide municipal-type services such as police protection, water, and sewage. In California the special district may perform only those functions set forth in the state enabling law. The city of Sacramento, however, under its home rule charter, has broader authority, covering "all municipal and police powers necessary to the complete and efficient administration of the municipal government, although such powers may not be herein expressly enumerated. . . ."[6]

These special districts have a greater claim on the citizen than does the county. Even though the county may provide some municipal services directly, and even though respect for county government has risen considerably in the past few years, the county government is not likely ever to command sufficient loyalty to create a "community." The citizen looks not to the county but to the special district that he joins with his immediate friends and neighbors for essential governmental services.

TABLE 1

Population of City of Sacramento and Sacramento County,
1850-1960

	County	Per cent of increase	City	Per cent of increase
1850	9,087		6,830	
1860	24,142	165.68	13,785	102.13
1870	26,830	11.13	16,283	18.12
1880	34,390	28.18	21,420	31.55
1890	40,339	17.30	26,386	23.18
1900	45,915	13.82	29,282	10.98
1910	67,806	47.80	44,696	45.81
1920	91,029	34.25	65,908	47.46
1930	141,999	55.99	93,750	42.24
1940	170,333	19.95	105,958	13.02
1950	277,140	62.70	137,572	29.83
1960	502,778	81.42	191,667	39.32

Source: United States Bureau of the Census.

OCCUPATIONS AND INCOME LEVELS

Sacramento's unique economic characteristics are important aspects of the metropolitan setting in the late 1950's. In California as a whole, manufacturing and trade combined account for about 45 per cent of total employment, with manufacturing slightly in the lead. Manufacturing employment is increasing most rapidly. Far behind come finance and government employment.[7]

In the Sacramento area, however, government employment and government-contract employment predominate. Together they account for over 40 per cent of total employment, with approximately 20,000 employees each in federal, state, and local government, and government-contract employment. Employment in wholesale and retail trade trails far behind in second place. Employment in service occupations follows and then manufacturing. The only other occupations providing sizable volumes of employment are transportation, communications, and utilities and contract construction. Much of the Federal government employment and the employment in manufacturing (Aerojet-General and Douglas Aircraft, for example) is related closely to military preparedness programs.[8] The income per household in Sacramento County, $7,408, ranks well above the California average of $6,950. In 1959 per capita income for California was $2,250 while in Sacramento County the figure was $2,319. The city of Sacramento has a higher income level—$2,646 per capita and $8,132 per household.[9]

Sacramento, then, is a "government city" with a relatively high income level. The economy of the city, and of the entire metropolitan area is dominated by governmental activity, either directly or indirectly.

PRESSURES FOR REORGANIZATION AND REFORM

THE *Sacramento Bee*

In September and October, 1955, the *Sacramento Bee*, the major metropolitan daily, carried a series of 19 lengthy articles on "Sacramento's Community Crisis." Some of the titles included: "Growth Makes Orphans of Cityless Fringes Bordering Sacramento," "Rising County Taxes, Assessments Plague Fringe

Area Dwellers," "Suburban Residents Find Little Independ-
ence in District Government," "Taxpayers Can Benefit from
Consolidation of Duplicating Functions," "Merger of City,
County as Fringe Problem Solution Merits Study," "Mass An-
nexation to Sacramento Is Proposed as Fringe Solution,"
"Citizens Commission Is First Step Toward Fringe, City
Solution."

The series painted an over-all picture of an "urbanopolis, a
lush jungle of subdivisions, shopping centers, commercial
strips, septic tanks, sewer lines. . . ." The plight of the fringe-
area residents, faced with heavier county taxation and increased costs for their municipal-type services, was described
and the city's more favorable financial position was stressed.

One article debunked the idea that residents of the unincorporated areas are more independent and have more "grass
roots" government than their neighbors in the city, noting the
unrepresentative character of district government. Various
schemes for providing better governmental services to the
suburbs—sale of services by the city, incorporation, urban
county services, functional consolidation, city-county merger,
etc.—were analyzed. Although the *Bee* favored mass annexation of suburban areas to the city of Sacramento, the concluding article called for the creation of a citizens' committee to
study the problem and recommend a proper solution.

The articles, together with a few *Sacramento Bee* editorials
on the subject, were combined into a free booklet entitled
Sacramento: A Crisis of Growth.

URBAN GOVERNMENT COMMITTEE OF THE GREATER
NORTH AREA CHAMBER OF COMMERCE

Even before 1960, when the Greater North Area Chamber of
Commerce became a part of the Sacramento City-County
Chamber of Commerce, the North Area organization claimed
to serve all of Sacramento County north of the American River.

James R. Cowan, who later played a prominent role both in the Sacramento Metropolitan Area Advisory Committee and in the Metropolitan Government Committee surveys, was president in 1955-1956 when the North Area chamber planned a program which included a study of the adequacy of local government in the North Area. The chamber created the Urban Government Committee; Mr. Cowan appointed the membership of the committee and assumed the chairmanship.

About two weeks after the *Bee* had published the final article in its series, Cowan proposed that certain kinds of questions and problems be studied:

> Shall the metropolitan North Area agree to systematic annexation by the city of Sacramento?
> Shall the unincorporated communities be encouraged to incorporate?
> Shall a "big city" be incorporated north of the American River? What are all the facts and aspects of incorporation as a solution?
> Shall a combined city-county government be considered?
> How should the city of North Sacramento grow?
> Is functional consolidation an answer?
> How can equitable representation be provided to all segments of the area under various proposals for governmental change?
> How can recommendations be best utilized for study by other community and civic groups?
> What are the legal problems and steps toward an orderly procedure for annexation and/or incorporation?[10]

While the Urban Government Committee did not find answers for many of these questions, it did issue a report, approximately ten months later (September, 1956), suggesting governmental arrangements for metropolitan Sacramento.[11] Detailed recommendations were avoided because of the work of the Sacramento Metropolitan Area Advisory Committee, the purpose of which was to make specific recommendations. Four interim conclusions were presented by the Urban Government Committee: a streamlined governmental unit, probably on a county-wide basis, should be supported by the North Area as a solution to the general problem; in any revised system of local government, representation should be on a community or area basis; flexible tax rates should be used in order to recognize the varying types and demands for municipal services in different areas; and until SMAAC completed its study, consolidation of districts with overlapping functions in the North Area and the county as a whole should continue.

SACRAMENTO AREA PLANNING ASSOCIATION

The Sacramento Area Planning Association was organized on October 19, 1953, apparently through the initiative of the League of Women Voters. The association disbanded in late 1959. The major objective of the Sacramento Area Planning Association was to promote planning in the Sacramento metropolitan area—recreation facilities, community beautification, traffic flow and parking, land use, and more efficient governmental units. The group was concerned about the political pressure and favoritism evident in zoning decisions and in the issuance of building permits; it called for a county master plan, reorganization of the tax structure, and more effective and influential planning commissions in the area.

The association sponsored discussions in 1956 of population growth and governmental problems in metropolitan Sacramento. A few of its members, some of whom were also members of the North Area's Urban Government Committee, advocated city-county merger.

SACRAMENTO COUNTY GRAND JURY

Considerable credit probably belongs to the grand jury for initiating major efforts at reorganizing local government in metropolitan Sacramento. The grand jury had been reporting upon unsatisfactory conditions over a period of several years— for example, in the 1953 report, the home for the aged, the Franklin road camp, and the county jail were criticized. The 1954 grand jury report dealt with the gross inadequacies in the county welfare department and the county civil service commission and personnel office. This report revealed some underlying reasons for the failure of the county welfare department to fulfill its responsibilities:

> Our examination has presented a picture of a county board of supervisors which has failed to recognize that Sacramento County has grown enormously within the past few years, and to take steps to meet the welfare problems that have increased with this growth. The Sacramento County Board of Supervisors, although responsible to the people for the conduct of the welfare department, have taken little active interest in and have been given little knowledge of the manner in which public assistance is administered in this county. . . .
>
> The information obtained from these two investigations just completed indicates to what extent our Board of Supervisors and several of our officials have failed to meet the responsibilities of their office. They have not recognized that Sacramento City and County have grown over the past several years into a large metropolitan area, or they have ignored this fact. . . .
>
> It is regrettable to find conditions existing in our county government such as enumerated in the two reports. It is especially regrettable that the taxpayer had to be put to the expense of two investigations to get facts the Supervisors should have known. . . .

The *Sacramento Bee,* in late February, 1955, called the grand jury report a devastating indictment of the administration of Sacramento County government and stated that a completely new concept of county government was needed. The year 1955 could be "a year of defeat or of unparalleled oppor-

tunity for the future of the 369,000 persons in the city and
county of Sacramento." Sacramento County, it stated, had one
of the finest county charters and yet was one of the worst run
counties in the state.

It is not possible to determine the precise degree to which
these several pressures for reorganization and reform caused
subsequent attempts at governmental change in the Sacramento metropolitan area. But altogether the *Bee* articles, the
activities of the Urban Government Committee, the urgings of
the Sacramento Area Planning Association, and the reports of
the grand jury constituted a persuasive call to action. Before
the year 1955 had come to a close, the decision to establish
the Sacramento Metropolitan Area Advisory Committee had
been made. In January, 1956, the committee began the task of
studying the problems of governmental organization in the
metropolis. Two years later SMAAC expired, the recommendations in its final report unfulfilled. The Metropolitan Government Committee was established to carry forward the study
of metropolitan Sacramento's governmental problems. During
the year and a half in which MGC worked, however, the metropolis experienced a movement to create a big new city northeast
of the city of Sacramento, a movement to annex to the city of
Sacramento a sizable area to the north (Hagginwood-Del Paso
Heights), and still another movement to annex a major area
to the northeast (Arden-Arcade) to Sacramento. In essence,
the SMAAC and MGC studies were phases of one continuous
effort, while the incorporation and two annexation movements
were separate attempts at governmental change. But in a real
sense each of these movements affected, and was affected by,
one or more of the others. In the end they were related actions
and reactions to the problem of government in metropolitan
Sacramento.

2

Citizens' Committees
For Metropolitan Study

SACRAMENTO METROPOLITAN AREA
ADVISORY COMMITTEE

At the October, 1955, organizational meeting of the Urban Government Committee of the Greater North Area Chamber of Commerce the difficulty of separating the North Area for study was discussed. A truly metropolitan study was needed. On October 26, 1955, the *Sacramento Bee* suggested that the mayor and city manager of Sacramento, the Sacramento county executive, and the chairman of the county board of supervisors constitute themselves a committee to study fringe-area problems. Approximately one week later the city council and the county board of supervisors agreed to establish a thirteen-member committee to study the problems of fringe areas and special districts in the county. Shortly, however, this plan was modified to provide for a larger committee (Sacramento Metropolitan Area Advisory Committee) to study the problems of

23

the entire metropolitan area. Nine members each were to be named by the city of Sacramento and by Sacramento County, and three members were to be named by North Sacramento.

The three participating governmental jurisdictions adopted a common resolution setting forth functional and organizational guidelines for SMAAC: to "study and make recommendations to interested public agencies regarding the broad problems of metropolitan area organization and growth, with attention to incorporation, the formation and/or consolidation of special districts, annexation or any other possible solution to the problems of governmental organization. The Committee shall act in an advisory capacity to the city councils and to the county board of supervisors." The resolution authorized the expenditure of funds that might be appropriated and the employment of consultants, and provided that certain local public officials serve as "ex-officio consultant members."[1]

By mid-January, 1956, all three jurisdictions had appointed their members. Selected from a list of 41 nominees given by councilmen and by civic, professional, and business organizations to represent the city of Sacramento were:

> A field representative for the State Board of Equalization, and president of the county employees union (H. E. Johnson)
> A member of the executive board of the Sacramento Women's Council and former chairman of the Sacramento City Planning Commission (Mrs. Arnold Waybur)
> A physician and board member of the County Medical Society (Orland Wiseman)
> An attorney and member of the Sacramento City Employees Retirement Board (Philip C. Wilkins)
> An attorney and member of the Sacramento City Transit Authority (Alvin Landis)
> An attorney who had just been defeated in the election for city council (Kneeland H. Lobner)

A partner in a large local real estate firm and past president of Sacramento Junior Chamber of Commerce (Thomas W. Yeates)

An administrative official of Sacramento State College (H. J. McCormick)

The owner of a large general construction company (Milton J. Heller)

Sacramento County representatives, chosen from the unincorporated area of the county, included:

A superintendent of a large elementary school district (James R. Cowan)

A business manager of a construction and general laborers' union (Percy F. Ball)

A president of a large general trucking concern (A. F. Dredge, Jr.)

A real estate subdivider and former president of the Sacramento Real Estate Board (Roland Federspiel)

An attorney (Edward McDonell)

A partner in a real estate firm (Fred W. Speich)

An attorney (John J. Wells)

An investment broker and resident partner of a brokerage firm (Edwin Witter)

Manager of the local Campbell Soup Company plant (V. A. Glidden)

There is no specific information on how the county representatives were selected. Except for Glidden, who moved out of the area in 1957 and was replaced by Elmer E. Nelson, of Aerojet-General Corporation, the city and county members remained constant throughout the life of smaac.

Only one of North Sacramento's original representatives on smaac served to the end, and the manner of their selection is not known. Signing the final smaac report for North Sacramento were:

A proprietor of a men's clothing store (Sammy Powell)

An owner of a motor parts company (J. H. Lanphier, Jr.)

The president of a large general construction company
(Frank Erickson)

How did SMAAC get started? Who initiated action? Why did
they think something should be done? Eight individuals involved in SMAAC were interviewed at length and their
responses to such questions varied in interpretation but indicated general agreement that the *Sacramento Bee* was a prime
mover in bringing about action. They said, in effect, that the
Bee articles, in pinpointing the problems of the metropolitan
area, caused the council and board of supervisors to take
action. Comments ranged from "appointment of SMAAC was a
way to stop other action which they [the boards] could not
control" to the observation that the *Bee* articles forced the
governing boards to give up their reluctance to act. In fact,
one of the *Bee* articles in the "Crisis of Growth" series recommended the establishment of a citizens' study committee on
metropolitan problems. A few individuals gave credit to the
Sacramento Area Planning Association and the Greater North
Area Chamber of Commerce Urban Government Committee
for sparking initial interest from which the *Bee* took its cue.

In the mid-1950's, the *Bee* articles had presented the only
comprehensive identification of governmental and economic
problems of the area. They alone made specific recommendations for the appointment of a study committee and clearly
assigned responsibility for action to the Sacramento city council and the Sacramento county board of supervisors. There is
no evidence that any action would have been taken then or in
the foreseeable future without this impetus.

While the Sacramento city council received nominations
from a variety of sources for its appointees to SMAAC, the interviewees did not know what procedure had been followed in
North Sacramento and Sacramento County. The members evidently were not selected to reflect a particular point of view,

either that of the selecting body or of the public. None of those interviewed admitted knowing of any persons or groups who "unofficially" advised the appointing bodies. A few interviewees felt, however, that SMAAC membership did not constitute a cross section of community leaders, particularly of community leaders from the city of Sacramento.

Those interviewed reported that there was little community-wide interest shown in the activities of SMAAC. Several organizations that had had a long-time interest in metropolitan affairs followed SMAAC's work. Both the League of Women Voters and the Sacramento Area Planning Association were represented at most SMAAC meetings. The Sacramento City-County Chamber of Commerce, the Greater North Area Chamber of Commerce, and the Junior League were said to have shown interest. The interviewees knew of no overt opposition to SMAAC's efforts until the final report was issued.

INITIAL ORGANIZATION AND OPERATION OF SMAAC

The first meeting of SMAAC was held on February 1, 1956. James R. Cowan was elected temporary chairman, and Thomas W. Yeates was elected temporary secretary. Both were later named to the permanent posts, along with a vice-chairman, Fred W. Speich. A steering committee, consisting of the officers plus four others appointed by the chairman, was authorized to propose organizational and procedural changes as the work of SMAAC progressed.[2]

The interviewees without exception emphasized the "hands off" policy taken by the three governmental bodies with regard to SMAAC's choice of officers, its procedures, and its final decisions. They also stressed that there was a minimum of internal politics among the SMAAC membership. Since the meetings were public and the press was always present, most SMAAC news was straight reporting. The chairman sent out only a small number of press releases. The chairman was, in effect, the official spokesman for the group and he made most of the public speeches regarding SMAAC and its work.

Although the resolution creating SMAAC authorized the employment of consultants, no funds were provided. The major financial assistance ultimately given by the sponsoring governments, $67,000, was used for the work of an outside consultant.

CONTRACT WITH PUBLIC ADMINISTRATION SERVICE

During its early orientation meetings SMAAC heard local officials speak on the problems and services of their jurisdictions. The central question in these meetings, as reported by several interviewees, was whether SMAAC should be an active study group and gather and weigh evidence, debate alternatives, and make findings and recommendations, or whether it should delegate the study, analysis, and recommendations to a consulting staff and act only as judges of whether these recommendations ought to be accepted, rejected, or modified. The most serious difference of opinion within SMAAC arose over this question.

In an orientation meeting a speaker from the University of California (Berkeley) recommended that SMAAC employ a consulting firm and then decide as to the general orientation and objectives of the consultant's work. SMAAC should keep in close contact with the survey group, review its work, make all decisions resulting from the survey, and work for the adoption of whatever recommendations might result.[3]

In early April a subcommittee appointed for the purpose presented the names of five firms or individuals who might be considered for employment as consultants. Only Public Administration Service and Harold Wise and Associates accepted the invitation to bid on the survey. These firms made their presentations to SMAAC on May 9, and the Public Administration Service was chosen for the job by a secret ballot vote of 13 to 3.

On May 15, 1956, the steering committee and PAS worked out a $67,000 proposal for the study, $55,000 of the amount being allocated for salaries. The PAS agreed to study existing governments in metropolitan Sacramento; to analyze existing governmental services, costs, and modes of financing; and to make recommendations for improvement. It would issue a final report within about ten months after the beginning of the survey. The contract, between PAS and the three sponsoring governments, was soon approved. The city of Sacramento and the county each agreed to pay 49 per cent of the total, and North Sacramento was to pay the remaining 2 per cent.

SMAAC's relationship to the work of the PAS and to the metropolitan government problem in general was not clear in the contract, and, in fact, was never worked out satisfactorily. SMAAC itself did comparatively little by way of actual study. About three months after the survey started, the chairman of SMAAC complained about poor attendance at meetings. Members did not want to come to meetings just to approve minutes of the previous meeting. "We've got to have some meat."[4] Even when PAS was about to issue its final report, SMAAC members disagreed over the role of the committee in handling the report.

SMAAC AT WORK

SMAAC met regularly, usually once a month, while the PAS was making its survey. In addition to the steering committee, which was active in guiding the group throughout, SMAAC created an aims and objectives committee and a public relations committee. PAS worked apart from SMAAC in developing the survey report although the PAS group reported from time to time on what other metropolitan areas had done or were doing to solve problems similar to those of Sacramento. There is nothing in SMAAC minutes or in the newspapers to indicate that PAS discussed or gave a preview of its findings and recommendations to the committee.

SMAAC deliberated over whether all changes in governmental structure should be discouraged until the PAS report had been completed. SMAAC went on record at its April meeting as opposing the incorporation of any new municipalities or the formation of any new community service districts until SMAAC's work had been completed. It opposed any annexations "to existing cities of established communities," but not necessarily all annexations. When the problem arose again in later meetings, some members did not oppose "normal growth patterns" but did want to "prevent the formation of islands of development that will make any final solution to our metropolitan problem impossible." In November, 1956, SMAAC continued to oppose new incorporations, but decided not to take a stand on other specific governmental changes because of "the present danger of misinterpretation of any stand the Committee might take."

SMAAC's public relations committee suggested the development of a Metropolitan Information Panel which would mobilize civic organizations in support of the final recommendations. But the Metropolitan Information Panel never became an effective organization, mainly because it was undertaken too late. As a result, no organized support existed after PAS had completed its survey and SMAAC had been disbanded.

Poor attendance by a few members caused SMAAC some concern. The North Sacramento representatives were particularly lax and were sent written reminders of their responsibility. SMAAC apparently did not resort to the extreme measures set out in its rules—that any member who failed to attend three consecutive meetings without cause was automatically dropped from the membership.

PAS FINAL REPORT

Two preliminary reports were issued by the PAS before its final report was made. The first, released November 13, 1956, gave details of the fact-finding project, which was almost complete. It dealt with the number of governmental units in Sacramento County and gave an analysis of the special districts in the county.[5] In the second report, released on February 19, 1957, the costs for governmental services, based on total local taxes and service charges, were compared for a standard house in the city of Sacramento and for one situated in each of six communities outside the city. The taxes and service costs were greater for all of the six communities. A second part of the report discussed the advantages and disadvantages of various possible governmental arrangements for metropolitan areas in general, but there was no statement as to what the PAS would recommend for metropolitan Sacramento.[6]

On May 22, 1957, PAS presented its final report to SMAAC and the public. During preceding months there had been much debate over how and to whom the report should be made. The uncertain relationship between SMAAC and PAS was clearly reflected in this disagreement over procedure. Some of the committee members felt that PAS should keep them informed of the progress and direction of its work so that the final recommendations of SMAAC would be coordinated with those of the consultant they had employed. Others wanted PAS to be free of any influence, even that of SMAAC. The latter group prevailed and the committee agreed that, since under contract PAS was solely responsible for its findings, SMAAC should not know details of the survey until the final report was made public.

This decision was made on February 19, 1957, but the man-

ner of presentation was debated by SMAAC members, and also
by newspaper editors, right up to the eve of the presentation
of the report. At the March 19 meeting, SMAAC adopted a
motion that "there shall be no formal presentation by PAS until
the report has been fully and freely discussed by the committee, and that PAS encumber the funds necessary for consultation
after discussion by the committee." In spite of this, the PAS
report was presented formally without any prior study by
SMAAC. The administrative assistant employed locally by PAS
kept the office open for several months thereafter, but no
further official consultation by PAS with SMAAC or local government officials took place.

As a concession to SMAAC, PAS agreed that city and county
officials should not be invited to the luncheon at which the
PAS report was presented. A number of SMAAC members decided that the presence of city and county officials would
"clothe the report with an aura of finality" and leave SMAAC
no choice but to accept the report. These public officials were,
of course, the official parties to the contract with PAS and had
appropriated the money to pay for the report.

In broad outline, PAS proposed a merger of the five incorporated municipalities and the county into a single unit—the
city-county of Sacramento—with the boundaries of the existing
county. This "metro" was to be divided into five boroughs: the
city of Sacramento would compose two boroughs; the unincorporated area to the north and east, two more; and the
remainder of the county, one. A metropolitan council composed of eleven members serving four-year, staggered terms
would be chosen as follows: one councilman elected in each
of the boroughs and six others elected at large. A mayor
would be elected for a two-year term by the councilmen from
among their group. A metropolitan manager with complete
responsibility for the administrative side of the government

would be selected by the council. The manager's powers would be comparable to those of the city manager of Sacramento. Each borough would have an advisory council, which in time might assume some local responsibilities. Areas not receiving municipal-type services would be designated as rural service areas and would have lower tax rates than the rest of the metro.

The PAS consultants apparently felt confident that this major governmental change could be accomplished under existing constitutional provisions.[7] They relied upon a provision in the California constitution that permitted a city of at least 50,000 population to withdraw from the county, taking additional territory with it if desired, and set itself up as a new city-county. The report proposed that the city of Sacramento withdraw from Sacramento County and take the remainder of the county with it. But PAS expressed some uncertainty over the legal basis for this drastic change: "Added guidance on constitutionality and on the proper legal procedures for consolidation should be secured by the Sacramento Metropolitan Area Advisory Committee from the sources already mentioned [Sacramento City Attorney, Sacramento County Counsel, State Legislative Counsel] and from the Attorney General. All possible legal doubts should be quickly resolved." Nevertheless, the legal discussion on consolidation concluded on this optimistic note: "If the people of Sacramento want metropolitan government it is not likely that the state legislature, special interest groups, local officials, or any combination of factors will prevent their realization of this goal."

Most local government officials, when asked by newsmen for their reactions to the PAS plan, avoided taking a stand. They believed in principle in the merits of consolidation, but they could not pass judgment on the specific recommendations until they had read the PAS report carefully. The *Sacramento Union*—an independent morning daily in the Sacramento metropolitan area having a total circulation of about one-third that of the *Bee*—reported the reaction of a councilman of North Sacramento. He was quoted as saying, "I have always been against any consolidation, as I don't believe we would benefit in any way beyond what we have now." The mayor pro tempore of Isleton, quoted in the *Sacramento Bee*, said, "I think it's all right for the metropolitan area up there, but I don't go for it for Isleton, 40 miles removed from the scene of activities. We certainly can't be said to benefit this far down here. From what I've seen of it, I don't like it." These were the only direct statements positively rejecting the PAS proposal at this stage.

Various groups immediately undertook to study the PAS report. The Urban Government Committee of the Greater North Area Chamber of Commerce pointed out that the PAS recommendations were similar to the previous suggestions of their group. The Arden-Arcade District Council of Improvement Clubs and the Carmichael Chamber of Commerce also appointed committees to study the report.

SMAAC AND THE PAS REPORT

While SMAAC decided not to study the PAS report before its release to the general public, it did not intend to "rubber stamp" the recommendations. Those members of SMAAC who wanted to study the report did convince the group that, after release of the PAS report, a few days should be allowed for individual study by SMAAC members. A series of meetings for more detailed study would follow.

Before considering what occurred in those meetings, it may be well to review the elapsed time since the decision to create SMAAC in late 1955. SMAAC held its first meeting on February 1, 1956. By mid-May, 1956, arrangements had been completed for employing the Public Administration Service, which made a report one year later, in May, 1957.

At the presentation luncheon the chairman reminded SMAAC members that the report was a research project first of all: "The committee will go into every single phase of it before deciding its recommendations." On May 27, 1957, SMAAC began a series of meetings on the PAS report. One member proposed that the group begin by voting general approval of the PAS plan, subject to later modifications of specific details, but a majority insisted that this would be premature. The group then turned to the issue that proved to be a major stumbling block for the PAS plan—the legal question of how the plan could be put into effect. The procedure apparently favored by PAS and theoretically possible under existing constitutional provisions would fail upon an adverse vote in any one of the incorporated municipalities. It was soon clear that there would be an adverse vote in one or more of them. Consequently, the recommended procedure was never seriously considered. The state legislature could be asked to enact legislation to implement the authorization for city-county consolidation already contained in the constitution. However, because of constitutional restrictions upon special legislation, such a statute would have to be applicable to all communities in the state, and would undoubtedly be too controversial to win approval in both houses.[8] A legislative subcommittee was appointed to study the legal aspects.

As the weeks went by, SMAAC members became convinced that only an amendment to the state constitution could insure the adoption of the PAS plan.[9] The PAS report had mentioned a constitutional amendment as one method of securing legal authority for the metropolitan plan, but since the plan could be put into effect without change in either state law or state constitution, the PAS people hoped that "these longer procedures can be avoided. . . ." No serious effort to secure an amendment was ever made in the legislature.

During SMAAC's deliberations doubts arose over the legality of PAS's plan for urban and rural tax differential zones that would permit different tax rates depending on the services received. In June, 1957, when SMAAC asked for an opinion regarding the constitutionality of such zones, the county counsel declared they were unconstitutional. The city attorney gave the same opinion and California's state attorney general concurred in a ruling on October 1, 1957.[10] SMAAC ultimately decided to ask for a constitutional amendment authorizing such special tax zones.

In addition to the legal obstacles, the group discussed whether it should approve the plan in principle or wrestle with specific details. One faction argued that SMAAC should use the report as a basis for preparing a detailed plan of government for metropolitan Sacramento. Other members felt that a charter commission ought to be allowed to work out the details. The issue was never really resolved.

SMAAC's own report, 12 printed pages approved on September 11, 1957, presented a brief history of its organization, followed by a summary of the PAS recommendations. SMAAC expressed agreement in principle with nearly all of the recommendations, but raised objection to having the membership of the first metro council chosen from the present members of the legislative bodies of the city of Sacramento, Sacramento County, and North Sacramento. In spite of this and other specific differences, the SMAAC report stated that matters of detail should be left to a charter commission.

To implement the PAS plan, SMAAC recommended a state constitutional amendment that applied only to Sacramento County. Under this amendment city-county merger could be adopted by a county-wide majority vote. It also should authorize varying tax rates based upon differences in services. In the meantime, an unofficial charter commission, appointed by the county and the five incorporated municipalities, should undertake at once to draft a proposed charter for the new metropolitan government which would be ready for consideration by the voters as soon as the constitutional amendment had been adopted. The amendment would give a permanent legal basis to the unofficial charter commission. SMAAC would extend beyond January 1, 1958, so that it could assist with the drafting of the constitutional amendment.[11]

On November 12, 1957 (about two years after it had been created), SMAAC presented this final report to the officials of the city of Sacramento, Sacramento County, and North Sacramento. Representatives from Folsom, Isleton, and Galt were also invited. One hundred fifty interested citizens attended the meeting. According to the minutes, the audience was equally divided between persons from within and from outside Sacramento city.

The minutes of this meeting are brief. Presentation talks were made by several SMAAC members, and there were questions from the officials and the audience concerning water, schools, and taxes. The chairman of the county board of supervisors, the mayor of Sacramento, and the mayor of North Sacramento, in commending SMAAC on its work, promised study and some sort of action on the part of the governments they represented. They suggested a joint meeting of the three governments about December 1 to consider the SMAAC final report further and to decide whether the life of SMAAC should be extended.

POPULAR REACTION TO THE PAS PLAN

Few positive rejections of the PAS plan were expressed immediately after its release; neither had there been strongly expressed approval. During the six months that SMAAC was studying the plan, the newspapers of the Sacramento area were strongly supporting it. The *Bee* evidently preferred mass annexation plus functional consolidation, but gave the PAS plan much publicity and insisted editorially that the people should have the opportunity of voting upon it. The *Union,* which had not given as much attention to metropolitan problems and proposals for change as the *Bee,* supported the PAS plan in editorials. The community newspapers and the shoppers' news publications of the general Sacramento area were enthusiastic about the plan.

Several organizations in the county also favored the plan. The Urban Government Committee of the Greater North Area Chamber of Commerce, which had studied the PAS plan during this period, presented a resolution to SMAAC endorsing the plan, subject to certain modifications. The Urban Government Committee continued throughout the remainder of its own existence to voice support for the PAS plan. Support also was given by the Carmichael Chamber of Commerce, which helped to sponsor essay contests on the PAS proposals in the area's schools. The Sacramento Area Council of Chambers of Commerce requested that the board of supervisors approve the PAS plan. According to a survey made by the *Sacramento Union,* only the Isleton Chamber of Commerce among the chambers in the area had taken a stand in opposition to the PAS plan.[12] The League of Women Voters in the area voted approval of the plan.

There was no evidence, however, of support from the public in general. The average citizen did not seem to feel that there were serious problems to be considered or that any action or change was needed. Very little support for the PAS plan came from public officials. Most county and municipal officials spoke only in general terms and avoided committing themselves, although a few went on record in opposition to the plan. Only one of Sacramento County's three representatives in the state legislature was willing to introduce the proposed amendment in the legislature. He would do this only if SMAAC, the county board of supervisors, and the city councils of all five municipalities made such a request.[13] At the public meeting in which SMAAC's final report was presented, one of the Sacramento County legislators was heard to say to a representative from one of the smaller cities: "Don't you worry. We'll kill this —— —— thing!"[14]

In November, about one month before SMAAC officially ceased to exist, the Interim Committee on Municipal and County Government of the state assembly held a one-day hearing on the SMAAC-PAS proposals to decide what state legislation should be proposed. No action was taken, and the view of the assembly committee was perhaps best expressed in this statement made by one of its members, a representative from the Sacramento area:

> . . . I believe that the members of the Committee [SMAAC] who were here today have benefited a great deal by the questions you have asked, and I think that it makes them realize all the more the inadequacy of the study that they have come up with at the present time. In other words, it is quite obvious that considerable more study must be given to the problem, and the details that can't be assumed to be filled in later on. . . . The details have got to be presented in the plan at the time the plan is submitted to this committee, or submitted to either the City Council of Sacramento, North Sacramento, or the County Board of Supervisors.[15]

SMAAC IS DISSOLVED

Within two or three days after SMAAC's final report, the *Sacramento Bee* polled the members of the county board of supervisors, the Sacramento city council, and the North Sacramento city council, asking whether they favored extending the life of SMAAC. A majority of the supervisors and Sacramento city councilmen indicated that they did. North Sacramento councilmen would not comment. The North Sacramento city council, on November 18, voted unanimously to cut its ties with SMAAC as of January 1. The city council had no "functional right" to approve a plan under which persons not residing in the city could vote the city out of existence. Further, the council had received no direction from the voters of North Sacramento.

The chairman of SMAAC at first stated that North Sacramento's action came as no surprise. North Sacramento sentiment had consistently been against any plan of governmental reorganization that would modify its status as an independent city. He pointed to the poor attendance record of North Sacramento's representatives to SMAAC. The next day, however, the chairman announced that negotiations were under way to compromise the differences between North Sacramento and SMAAC. The proposed constitutional amendment would contain a provision that the governmental merger would apply to Sacramento and to North Sacramento only after "a majority of the electorate in each city voted approval."[16]

In the meantime, Sacramento County and the city of Sacramento continued to weigh the question of SMAAC's future. On November 25 the county board of supervisors voted that all of the requests for continuation of SMAAC be "taken under advisement." One supervisor stated that a new committee might be created in place of SMAAC to draft the necessary laws and constitutional amendments. On November 26, representatives of SMAAC met with the Sacramento city council to discuss the future of SMAAC. SMAAC's chairman made a case for SMAAC's continuation and suggested that another advisory group be appointed to make "a two or three year study of charter provisions for the new government." The city council decided that it should have another meeting with SMAAC and also a joint meeting with the county board of supervisors before arriving at a decision.

Some SMAAC members disagreed with the chairman and felt that SMAAC had outlived its usefulness and should be disbanded. It would be futile, they said, to expect "the political boys in office," who traditionally oppose governmental change, to favor SMAAC's continued existence.[17]

When the Sacramento city council met with SMAAC representatives on December 9, the council postponed decision. The county board of supervisors and representatives of North Sacramento, Folsom, Galt, and Isleton were invited to the next council meeting, on December 18, to decide the issue. The fate of SMAAC seemed to have been settled already. SMAAC representatives spoke in terms of a smaller committee. Sacramento's mayor and its city manager talked more and more about a new committee. The manager wanted to be sure that any new committee would not keep the sponsors in the dark until the issuance of a final report.

At the December 18 meeting, continuation of SMAAC received slight consideration, even though the majority of county supervisors and the Sacramento city councilmen had recently gone on record in favor of the continuation of SMAAC. A new committee composed of 15 members representing Sacramento County, the city of Sacramento, North Sacramento, Folsom, Galt, and Isleton was to be formed. The Sacramento county board of supervisors, Sacramento city council, and four Isleton city councilmen present agreed that the new committee should study only the merger plan and "problems related to it." Representatives of Folsom, Galt, and North Sacramento said they would take the matter before their full councils before announcing a stand. One newspaper reporter interpreted the Isleton vote as "the first crack in the wall the smaller cities were setting up against any change of the county's government structure."[18]

When the Sacramento Metropolitan Area Advisory Committee went out of existence, no action had been taken on its recommendations by the sponsoring governmental bodies. In the months intervening between SMAAC's final report and the committee's demise, it became clear that neither the city of Sacramento nor Sacramento County was going to press for further consideration of the SMAAC-PAS plan. They apparently felt that there was little community support for a consolidated government and that the legal and procedural obstacles to forming such a government were indeed imposing. City-county merger meant the death of the larger cities and seemed to have no advantages for the smaller, more rural communities of Isleton and Galt. The governing bodies probably would have preferred to let SMAAC's report lie without action of any kind. At the same time, the local newspapers were constantly reminding them that they had spent $67,000 of tax money for the report. It could hardly be ignored or swept under the civic rug. Their solution to this problem was typically American—form a new committee.

FORMATION OF THE METROPOLITAN GOVERNMENT COMMITTEE

On December 27, 1957, the Sacramento city council approved a resolution creating the Metropolitan Government Committee (MGC). Sacramento County was to be represented on MGC by the county executive plus four members appointed by the county board of supervisors and living in the unincorporated areas. The city manager plus four city residents appointed by the city council would represent the city. North Sacramento's city manager plus one person appointed by its city council were made members, and the city councils of Folsom, Galt, and Isleton were to appoint one member each. The original resolution provided that four of Sacramento County's members and four members from the city of Sacramento must be former members of SMAAC. The city council made this permissive and set a termination date for MGC of June 30, 1959.[19]

As finally adopted by the county board of supervisors and the cities of North Sacramento, Isleton, Galt, and Folsom, the resolution stated that the creation of MGC was not to be construed as an endorsement of SMAAC's recommendations, and that membership was to be made up of six persons each from Sacramento County and the city of Sacramento, two each from Folsom, Isleton, and Galt, and three from North Sacramento. The duties and responsibilities of MGC were stated as follows:

> It shall study the problems of government in the Sacramento Metropolitan Area and possible solutions to those problems, including the recommendations made by the Public Administration Service and the Sacramento Metropolitan Area Advisory Committee.
>
> It shall keep the respective City Councils and the Board of Supervisors regularly informed through quarterly reports concerning the progress of its studies, and shall take such other appropriate means to keep the Councils and the Board of Supervisors informed as it may deem necessary and proper.
>
> It shall act only in an advisory capacity to the respective City Councils and the Board of Supervisors.
>
> It shall not officially represent the City Councils and the Board of Supervisors unless specifically authorized.

"Metropolitan Area" was defined as including all of the county of Sacramento. Any legislation, or constitutional amendment, that MGC felt was necessary should be prepared and submitted to the governing bodies of areas affected for their consideration. Unless specifically authorized by all of the governing bodies in the county, MGC could not recommend such legislation or constitutional amendment to other legislative bodies or to other organizations.

The cost of MGC was to be shared equally by Sacramento County and the city of Sacramento. The four smaller municipalities were to pay nothing. All fiscal matters were to be handled by the appropriate officers of the Sacramento County government. MGC's operation was under the strict control of the city of Sacramento and the county. All of the sponsoring governments could strongly influence its conclusions.

Four of Sacramento County's representatives on MGC had been members of SMAAC: James R. Cowan, Elmer E. Nelson, Fred W. Speich, and Thomas W. Yeates. The two other members named by the county were a rancher and former state assemblyman who was also a member of the county board of education, Dwight Stephenson, and the county executive, M. D. Tarshes. The Sacramento city council, on January 30, 1958, approved the amended resolution and named its six members. Four of these had been members of SMAAC: Milton J. Heller, Alvin Landis, H. J. McCormick, and Philip C. Wilkins. Also named were an assistant general manager of the Sacramento Municipal Utility District, Carl L. Richey, and the city manager, Bartley W. Cavanaugh. North Sacramento named an investment firm executive, R. O. Mapes; an architectural draftsman and member of the city planning commission, Malcolm O. Mau; and the city manager, Homer H. Jack. Folsom selected Marjorie Handy, a member of its city council, and the city attorney, Louis A. Boli. A retired canning firm employee, Emil Evers, and a member of the city council, Emil Schock, represented Galt. Isleton named the city superintendent of schools, Alwyn Amerman, and an oil company representative, Glenn L. Maxey. Nineteen of the 21 persons originally appointed to MGC signed the final report. Elmer E.

Nelson of Sacramento County, who resigned before work of MGC was completed, was succeeded by Percy F. Ball, a former member of SMAAC who remained to sign the final MGC report. Marjorie Handy from Folsom attended some of the early meetings, but did not participate in MGC activities thereafter or sign the final report.

Cowan, SMAAC's chairman, expressed reservations about what he viewed as the overrepresentation of the small cities. Although these cities had a total population of only 16,000, nine out of the 21 members came from them.

> This will definitely weaken the committee. It's not that the small cities shouldn't have the right to speak their piece, but I don't believe the bare fact that a community is incorporated should give it that much larger voice. . . . How about Arcade with its 45,000 people, or Carmichael with 26,000 or North Highlands with more than 20,000? This is a basic injustice to the proposal.[20]

At the final meeting of SMAAC, less than a week later, the SMAAC chairman seemed to have reconciled himself to the membership arrangement. He said: "In thinking about this, it seems to me that the small cities have been a big hurdle for our merger plan and perhaps it will be easier to adjust their problems into the plan if they have this large number of representatives."[21]

Thirteen members of MGC were interviewed. Most stated categorically that MGC was the idea of either the Sacramento city council or the Sacramento County board of supervisors or both. Most also believed that a general dissatisfaction with SMAAC's report had spurred these official bodies to act. SMAAC had been "99 per cent theory—not practicable." "Insufficient attention had been given to alternatives to city-county consolidation, and a further review was needed." "Consolidation was impossible without a constitutional amendment and the smaller cities were opposed to it." One interviewee thought that the county board had strongly supported the creation of MGC because, although it favored consolidation, the supervisors wanted the county to play a more important role than that outlined in the SMAAC-PAS plan. The city and the county of Sacramento were still under pressure from the newspapers to justify the $67,000 spent for the SMAAC report. Something had to be done. One person, thoroughly disillusioned, said, "The last step in killing off SMAAC and the easiest was—study it to death."

There was no evidence from the interviewees that community opinion was widely solicited in selecting the MGC members. The selection of some former SMAAC members was to be expected. Participation by city and county officials in all of MGC's activities should avoid recurrence of the lack of liaison between the committee and the sponsoring bodies, as had been the case with SMAAC, and so the appointment of the two city managers, a city attorney, and the county executive was not surprising. Views expressed at various stages of the interviews emphasized that representatives of the small municipalities participated in MGC simply to insure that their autonomy and power of self-determination would in no way be infringed. The fact that most of these people did not play an active role indicates that they were satisfied that the interests of their cities were not in danger or that they did not believe the problems being discussed were their concern.

The respondents noted a general lack of interest in MGC's work among organizations and interest groups. The League of Women Voters, the Sacramento Area Planning Association, the chambers of commerce, the Junior League, and a few other groups sent representatives to the meetings from time to time, but no direct support was given to MGC as such. Most of these organizations were committed to follow the study because of their previous interest and work toward some kind of area-wide planning. As for opposition, two respondents stated that the Urban Government Committee of the Greater North Area Chamber of Commerce was basically opposed to MGC's work and conclusions. The Urban Government Committee had gone on record as favoring SMAAC's plan for city-county consolidation and was suspicious of, if not opposed to, MGC's work, which might not approve or effectively implement the merger. Two respondents cited the opposition of local, nonmunicipal fire departments to MGC's desire to push for mass annexation and consolidation of functions. Such actions would have brought an end to many of these small departments. Generally, MGC attracted lukewarm support, at best, from outside organizations, and some potentially strong opposition from others.

EARLY WORK OF MGC

The first meeting of MGC was held February 19, 1958. After election of temporary officers—all of whom were formerly members of SMAAC and were later named to the permanent posts—and the decision to meet semimonthly, the meeting was given over to general discussion. The county executive expressed the hope that members of MGC would not approach their assignment with fixed opinions about the SMAAC proposals or about any other proposals for governmental reorganization. One member suggested that MGC should get experts and also the public into its discussions.[22]

As with SMAAC, organizational and procedural decisions of the committee were arrived at by democratic processes in public meetings. The interviewees stressed that there was a minimum of internal politics among the members. The sponsoring governmental bodies maintained the same "hands off" policy during MGC's life, but the membership on MGC of the appointed executives of the county and the two largest cities created a significant difference between MGC and SMAAC. While the influence of these executives is impossible to assess with precision, there is little doubt that the effect of the presence of the Sacramento city manager and the county executive was important. The press attended all meetings of MGC and its activities were fully reported. The chairman gave occasional press releases, and in this sense he was MGC's official spokesman.

Sacramento County paid all of MGC's expenses and billed the city of Sacramento for its proportionate share. The total cost of MGC was approximately $20,000. None of those interviewed felt that MGC's work was inadequately financed or was not given proper support by the city and the county of Sacramento.

A study program of MGC was discussed at the second meeting. Assessment and collection of taxes, inequality of tax rates, duplication of services by special districts, and overlapping boundaries of special districts were considered, but the group did not agree on a program of study. The members decided to invite the Sacramento county planner, the Sacramento city planner, the chairman or some other member of the planning commissions of Sacramento County and the municipalities of Sacramento, North Sacramento, Folsom, and Galt, and the mayor of Isleton to their next meeting to discuss present and future plans for the total area.[23]

The minutes for the next five meetings show that MGC paralleled SMAAC in its early meetings. The group listened to representatives of various governmental agencies explain the nature and operations of their organizations. The meetings were poorly attended and, on one occasion, the chairman was instructed to write a letter to each member stressing the importance of attendance and promptness. After having heard from all of the representatives, MGC decided to hire a full-time research secretary. A subcommittee was appointed to determine the qualifications for the job and to screen the applicants.

INCORPORATION PROPOSAL INFLUENCES MGC

On the evening of June 17, 1958, a proposal to incorporate a large new city northeast of Sacramento, which is the subject of the next chapter, was made public. The ineffectiveness of MGC so far was certainly one of a number of reasons for this proposal. The MGC chairman announced a few days thereafter that he would recommend that MGC give immediate attention to a study of the advantages of separate incorporation of the northeast area versus the advantages of annexation to Sacramento. This recommendation was adopted on June 25. According to newspaper accounts, the chairman emphasized that MGC was not abandoning plans to study city-county merger and other reorganization possibilities, but that problems growing out of the incorporation movement now under way must be studied first. The committee planned to devote six months to this study. The Sacramento city manager promised to provide the needed cost figures.

In mid-August a research director was appointed. (He was forced to resign within a few months because of illness.) MGC was divided into four subcommittees, of which the county executive and the two city managers were ex officio members, to study incorporation versus annexation. The subcommittees held meetings throughout the summer. Their studies were based primarily on a comparison of costs of services under existing arrangements, under separate incorporation, and under annexation to the city of Sacramento.

In September the chairman repeated MGC's ultimate obligation to analyze and evaluate the SMAAC-PAS recommendations, even though the incorporation movement compelled the com-

mittee to give full attention to that for the time being. He
stated that if MGC decided to support city-county merger it
would be obligated to draft a constitutional amendment and
submit it to the respective governing bodies for consideration.
When it was brought out in subsequent discussion that about
90 per cent of the county's population was living in about 25
per cent of the county's area, someone suggested that perhaps
MGC should concern itself only with this 25 per cent instead
of the entire county. In the light of MGC's final report, this
suggestion was prophetic.

The report on incorporation versus annexation was submitted to MGC at its January, 1959, meeting, although the new
city incorporation effort had been abandoned in November.
The report concluded that separate incorporation, with a
level of services equal to that of the city of Sacramento, would
require a municipal property tax rate of $2.26 in the new
municipality. In the case of mass annexation an over-all municipal property tax rate of only $1.73 would be needed to
achieve a uniform level of services. Present city taxpayers
would pay about two-thirds of the cost of raising the level of
services in the northeast area. Over a period of years, however,
the taxpayers of the central city would benefit from increased
land valuation in the northeast area.[24] The report was given
to a subcommittee for further study, corrections, and revisions.
In a meeting on February 4, 1959, this subcommittee decided
to recommend mass annexation of all of the area expected to
be urban in character by 1980. County and city planners
would draw the exact boundaries, but not, as suggested by
some, the boundaries for "stage annexations" also. Folsom and
North Sacramento could join if they wished. The subcommittee
also agreed to recommend functional consolidation of city and
county services. The schools were left to the county committee
on school organization. In early March the subcommittee made

the additional recommendation that the Arden-Arcade annexation movement—begun late in 1958 and considered in a later chapter—be endorsed as an important step toward implementation of mass annexation.[25]

The subcommittee report was accepted in essence by MGC. The *Sacramento Bee,* in an editorial entitled "Big Annexation Proposal Best Meets the Realities" (March 6, 1959), argued that city-county merger was not feasible at present and the MGC plan offered those people now served by many special districts the opportunity to change to efficient, integrated government. The MGC plan does not kill merger, but is a logical step toward it. On April 1, the MGC chairman urged the Sacramento city council to get together with the county to study what governmental functions could logically be consolidated. The county board of supervisors had already instructed the county executive to undertake this determination on behalf of the county. Although one member of the county board of supervisors asked the board in April to go on record in favor of the MGC plan, the matter was not brought to a vote.

FATE OF MGC RECOMMENDATIONS

The final report of MGC, a document of only 31 pages, presents four alternative solutions to metropolitan area problems of government—separate incorporation, federation, city-county separation, and city-county consolidation. All are found unsatisfactory or unfeasible, although the report states that city-county consolidation may "ultimately be the best solution." The committee recommended action on its subcommittee's plan for mass annexation of the area expected to be urban in character by 1980 and for approval of the pending Arden-Arcade annexation. MGC also recommended concurrent studies by the city and county governing bodies leading to consolidation of such city-county functions as planning, tax assessment, recreation, sewers, road construction, storm drainage, and water. After enlargement of the city through mass annexation, a charter commission, representing all areas, should study the adequacy of the city charter under the new conditions.[26]

The *Sacramento Bee* called for action. After three years of study and at a cost of more than $70,000, a fair and feasible plan for the city and county had been developed. The pending Arden-Arcade annexation was a part of this plan. The city and county must show good faith by getting to work on functional consolidation. Two months later the *Bee* took the Sacramento city council to task for dragging its feet on this matter. A resolution to study the feasibility of functional consolidation was, upon introduction, simply referred to the city attorney for study. The *Bee* insisted that the council get at the business of functional consolidation in order to counter the "land grab" charges voiced by opponents of the Arden-Arcade annexation. The voters in Arden-Arcade needed to be assured that their annexation would be part of an over-all plan for the area. The election on the issue was only five weeks away.[27]

The Urban Government Committee still urged city-county merger, but the North Area chamber overrode its committee's negative recommendation and did finally endorse the Arden-Arcade annexation as a part of MGC's plan for functional consolidation. The Sacramento City-County Chamber of Commerce, although it had not been active in governmental reorganization efforts, endorsed the Arden-Arcade annexation early. The two chambers agreed to work to achieve annexation to the city of Sacramento of the remaining unincorporated areas of metropolitan Sacramento if the annexation succeeded. If the annexation was defeated, they would wait the 12-month period required by law and then cooperate to bring about mass annexation.

The overwhelming defeat of the Arden-Arcade proposal was

a serious blow to the entire MGC plan and to these incipient efforts by organizations to act upon governmental problems. The SMAAC and MGC plans have been revived periodically but never acted upon. On January 2, 1960, the *Sacramento Bee* printed an editorial stating that MGC recommendations cannot implement themselves. Since representatives of the city of Sacramento and of Sacramento County had signed the MGC report, a commission representative of both the city and the county should be set up to put the plan into action. The planning directors, the engineers, and the chief executives of the two governments were proposed as members of such a commission. Again in January, 1964, the executive officer of the newly created Sacramento County Local Agency Formation Commission indicated that the commission would probably give serious attention to SMAAC-MGC plans.[28]

SMAAC AND MGC
EVALUATED BY SELECTED MEMBERS

Why have the SMAAC-PAS plan and the MGC recommendations lain dormant? The 16 individuals close to the movement (five of whom served on both committees) who were interviewed almost unanimously cited lack of community support as a major reason. Several felt that more support from the city and county, from service clubs, chambers of commerce, neighborhood clubs, home builders and real estate groups, and from central political organizations all would have been helpful. A few felt that the lack of coordination among SMAAC, PAS, and the sponsoring bodies had discouraged support for the plan. Beyond this general recognition of lack of community-wide interest, the interviewees did not seem to be able to judge how much and from what source support for their work came. The *Bee*, they all agreed, was in favor of the SMAAC study, and most felt that the paper supported the work of MGC also. The editorial policy of the paper had always viewed mass annexation as the best solution to governmental problems.

Besides the *Bee,* the individuals in SMAAC and MGC seemed at a loss to pinpoint support. The schools were not concerned as long as the proposed changes did not affect them. Real estate people and downtown businesses generally were "passive," "disinterested," or "cautious." Two interviewees did mention that the Sacramento business group favored annexation. The attitudes of suburban businesses were not known. Several felt these enterprises were "receptive to change," or at least not opposed, while about the same number viewed that group as opposed to the MGC report because it might cost them money.

It was generally agreed that officials of all cities were opposed to the SMAAC-PAS plan. In the interviewees' minds, this attitude stemmed from their provincialism, "desire to protect financial interests of residents," and "fear of losing out by consolidation." Sacramento city officials were considered favorably disposed to less drastic MGC recommendations because they had finally realized that the city would have to take a prominent role in solving area-wide problems and in preventing the separate incorporation of the North Area. The interviewees varied widely in their evaluations of the county officials' attitudes to SMAAC and MGC—from "favorable—would be top dogs" to "negative" or "reserved—didn't even read the reports in some cases." Either there was a wide range of opinion among the county officials or the individuals interviewed interpreted the same actions in different ways. The League of Women Voters was seen by all questioned to be favorable to the SMAAC-PAS and the MGC proposal, although a few felt that most League members preferred city-county consolidation.

Although several respondents noted the lack of participation in the SMAAC and MGC movements of influential people in the Sacramento area, they could not identify who these people might be. They spoke of "important bankers and business people." These "influential people" were not involved because they could not see that a tangible problem existed. In addition, there were no established means for involving them—no distribution of information or effective use of communications media. One respondent recognized the underlying lethargy of government employees as holding down the development of effective community leaders and an active citizenry.

The interviewees found it easier to identify specific practical reasons for the failure of their movements to inspire effective action. The timing was poor in the case of SMAAC; its report was released just before a city council election in Sacramento. SMAAC should have established better public relations—perhaps employed a staff—and kept the community better informed. The sponsoring bodies should have been brought in on the final decision-making on recommended action. SMAAC was slanted toward outlying areas. The committee should have assigned subcommittees to study specific aspects of the report and not simply sat back and waited for a grand scheme to emerge in the final report. In fact, some felt that a consultant should not have been hired. PAS, they said, had little understanding of the community. It took an ivory tower approach and did not realize the attitude of the city and county; its recommendations threatened the existing power structure. As one individual said, "Keep the experts on tap, not on top." Another respondent felt, however, that "the climate for acceptance didn't exist to begin with."

Perhaps during SMAAC's work a climate congenial to governmental reorganization could have been created. One respondent felt that a daily paper in the northeast area that asked questions and took a straightforward approach would have helped a great deal to give citizens factual information on which to judge the issue. More participation by the public and wider publicity seemed to many persons a way of preventing the failure of SMAAC. One individual felt that the Metropolitan Information Panel was a good idea and should have had official backing.

A few persons involved in SMAAC felt personnel changes could have made a difference in SMAAC's fate. One called for a consultant board on city-county merger, using academicians and other resource persons. PAS, one interviewee said, did not demonstrate that the problems were real ones. The study should have been more "factual." One person thought that too many people on SMAAC made little or no contribution to the committee's work, inferring that the existing structure and membership of the organization might have been a stumbling block to effective action.

The same basic reasons—lack of support from the community or its generally acknowledged leaders, poor public relations and publicity—were cited by participants as causing the failure of MGC. Interestingly enough, two respondents thought the group should have been a citizens' committee, with experts available for advice, and complained that the city and county executives tended to dominate the committee and "dilute its effectiveness." "The officials are apathetic and they don't know too much about the problem." Some in SMAAC had felt that the exclusion of these officials from the committee's work had been a reason for its failure. Another from MGC felt that the study subcommittee approach used—and favored by some in SMAAC as an alternative to using experts—had not "made much of a contribution." Two thought that before another committee is formed, they ought to find out exactly what the community wants and what it is willing to do to obtain it. A few sharply criticized MGC membership for its apathy, for the poor attendance of representatives from small cities, and for its failure to be truly representative.

In general, the leaders of the movements felt that the SMAAC-PAS proposal was premature. The people did not see the need for change, did not know how they would be affected, and therefore did not see why established concepts of government ought to be disrupted. This general apathy, as the leaders called it, would have to be overcome before the public support, which was essential to the success of a reorganization movement, could be rallied. The work of a study committee in Sacramento such as SMAAC or MGC is, then, twofold. It must not only develop meaningful and practicable solutions to the problems it studies, but it must educate—and understand— the people whose problems it is considering.

CONCLUSIONS

Since the SMAAC and the MGC committees were the only two reorganization efforts that were sponsored and supported by existing governmental bodies—the others were founded and executed by private citizens—it seems most appropriate to conclude this chapter by exploring the implications of the SMAAC-MGC experience for questions of governmental sponsorship, and organizational structure and procedures. The kind of organization that is needed to bring about governmental change is revealed in part by locating the sources of motivation for change. If official governmental agencies are sincerely interested in governmental change, are willing to see the issue studied openly and objectively, and are willing to commit themselves to some kind of action, then those agencies ought to create, charter, and support a study group. If, on the other hand, the motivation for change arises outside the governmental structure, attempts may be made to arouse governmental agencies to appoint a study committee, or an independent group may be created that is committed to study and to bringing about change through political action. It is obviously easier, in almost any circumstances, to turn to government for creation and support of a study commission. If, as in Sacramento, agitation for change has not arisen from either government or a citizen group but from an institutional source such as a newspaper or a grand jury, the best and most feasible type of organization becomes a more troublesome problem. The constituted governmental authorities may feel that agitation is a direct attack on them rather than on the structure, and, while they may create a study commission, they are likely to be unsympathetic to the whole enterprise. This, in fact, seems to have been the case in Sacramento.

There are also important questions of employment and use of staff. SMAAC employed outside staff and the committee did not participate actively in the study. The members of MGC constituted themselves as study committees and wrote their own report. The weight of interviewee opinion favors the employment and full use of staff for fact-gathering, analysis, and reporting. Some MGC members showed marked dissatisfaction with its study procedure; the subcommittees had neither the time nor the competence to do their own staff work. A director of research, employed for a few months, was not adequate staff assistance. On the other hand, the even stronger criticism of the SMAAC-PAS relationship by participants indicates that when technical staff go beyond "fact-finding, analysis, and reporting" important problems of communication and authority can arise Neither the committee nor the community was kept informed of PAS's progress or findings until the final report was revealed. Since the local government legislative bodies, which had financially sponsored the study, learned only after completion of a final report that it recommended their own liquidation, it is not surprising that councilmen and members of the county board of supervisors greeted the recommendation with less than enthusiasm.

It is equally apparent that the SMAAC-PAS relationship inhibited the development of community support for the plan by its policy of keeping everyone in the dark until the issuance of the final report. The conclusion implied is that an effective study group hoping to bring about governmental changes should employ an adequate trained staff but should also study and understand the problems itself and keep in touch with the work of the staff. Perhaps one of the most important activities of the study committee is to act as liaison between the technicians and the community they represent, informing each of the work and opinions of the other.

Significantly, although most members of both SMAAC and MGC credited the failure of their organizations primarily to lack of community support, they did not seem to be aware of this or other problems prior to or during the life of their group. Only through hindsight did they recognize the depth of citizen apathy, or organizational problems, or problems of technical assistance. The interviews, conducted after the fact, tapped this new insight.

Anything like the SMAAC-PAS plan, of course, would present almost insurmountable legal and constitutional problems to any community. When this community cannot obtain essential support from its city and county officials and the public, the plan becomes impossible to achieve. The MGC plan also required this support. As long as Sacramento County views annexations to the city of Sacramento as encroachments on its own power and prestige, and as long as the city is similarly fearful of functional consolidation as a device to transfer control of governmental functions to the county, neither the SMAAC-PAS plan for city-county merger, nor MGC's recommendations for mass annexation, seem likely to be put into effect.

3

The New City
Incorporation Attempt

On June 17, 1958, a group known as the Citizens' Committee for Incorporation declared its intention to create a new 165-square-mile city, northeast of the city of Sacramento.[1] The area's estimated population of 150,000 was nearly equal to that of Sacramento, and it covered about five times as much territory as Sacramento. The committee's announcement occurred about five months after the last meeting of SMAAC and about four months after the first meeting of MGC.

Unknown to the public, discussion and preliminary planning for this move had begun late in 1957, paralleling the beginning of MGC. Its origins may have been nurtured much earlier, even before the Urban Government Committee of the Greater North Area Chamber of Commerce was formed. Members of the Carmichael Chamber of Commerce, many of whom also belonged to the Greater North Area chamber, historically have held an image of their community—a small unincorporated area about ten miles east of Sacramento—as a separate, rapidly growing, progressive community. They have sought to provide adequate governmental services for the area. In the early 1950's some citizens attempted to re-establish a community service utility district coterminous with the Carmichael fire district. This plan failed to gain the voters' approval, and some of the same citizens helped to form the Urban Government Committee of the Greater North Area Chamber of Commerce. Since the recommendations of this committee were similar to those subsequently presented in the SMAAC-PAS report, the Carmichael group—not all of whom were well known to each other—appeared willing to wait for action on the report during the summer of 1957. When city and county officials continued to delay action on the plan, this informal group turned to incorporation of the northeast area, of which Carmichael was only a small part, as a solution.

The informed citizens of Carmichael were aware of the serious nature of their local problems. The community is old. During the 1950's many of the four- and five-acre single-family lots and other larger acreages were subdivided. The numerous cesspools and open drainage ditches needed to be replaced by facilities that would provide more water and adequate sewage disposal. In addition, the county board of supervisors had allowed spot zoning for commercial purposes along the main thoroughfare, which bordered upper-middle-class homes on the south. Many considered the county maintenance of the roads and drainage system in the community entirely inadequate.

The final impetus for the 1958 incorporation attempt apparently grew out of informal conversations among members of the Carmichael Chamber of Commerce in late fall of 1957, after the SMAAC-PAS report had been all but shelved. Jack Moore, an insurance and investment broker and former president of the chamber, and Howard Craig, a retired general who had been a candidate for the governing board of the rejected utility district in Carmichael, were the first to take any action as individuals. In mid-January, 1958, they invited Carmichael resident Walter Isenberg, an employee of the State Department of Corrections, to lunch with them. Craig had recognized Isenberg's organizational abilities during his efforts in the utility district campaign. Jack Moore stated, "At this point we merely wanted to study our problems, but not again with the same people who had been working on them at the governmental level."

Some individuals in the movement reported a feeling expressed in the area that city-county merger could be attained through the "threat of incorporation," but Isenberg immediately took the view that if incorporation were attempted every effort should be made to insure success. At just what point the committee for incorporation as a whole accepted the view of incorporation as an end in itself is not entirely clear; apparently it became committee policy, although the members did not seem to agree unanimously on this point. This group first included only the Carmichael area in its plan for incorporation; then Arden was added, later Arcade; and finally, as new members were recruited to the study group, the area grew to 165 square miles. According to the minutes of the committee, the general boundaries had been agreed upon by the fourteenth of April, 1958 (see Map 3).

DEMOGRAPHIC SETTING

The population of the proposed new city in 1960 was 187,336.[2] The area was almost 99 per cent white, as compared with 87 per cent in the city of Sacramento. The population was comparatively young; most areas show a median age of about 25 years. By contrast, within the city of Sacramento the median

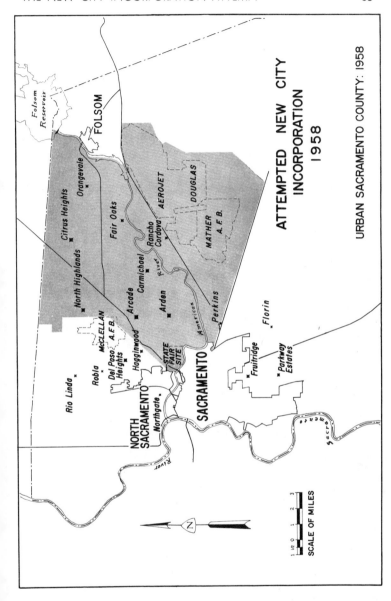

ATTEMPTED NEW CITY
INCORPORATION
1958

URBAN SACRAMENTO COUNTY: 1958

age exceeded 35 years in over one-half of the census tracts. Except for the Mather Air Force Base area, in which less than 3 per cent of the dwellings were occupied by the owner, owner-occupancy was registered at more than 62 per cent in most areas, exceeding the home ownership rate of 54 per cent in the city of Sacramento. In all but two of the United States census tracts within the proposed incorporation area, over 91 per cent of the houses were in sound condition. Only 85 per cent of the dwellings in the city were judged sound. It should be noted that the proposed new city contained large densely populated sections, but that it also contained much undeveloped land—particularly south of the American River.

LEADERSHIP

The incorporation movement was initiated and promoted by representatives of Carmichael. Only two of the 14 men who signed the letter of invitation to the first public meeting in June were outsiders. In late May, after much of the planning had been completed, David Yorton, chairman of the Arden-Arcade Council of Improvement Clubs, and Guy Fairchild, chairman of the Arden-El Camino park district board, joined the committee. They were to represent the Arden-Arcade area, the heavily populated territory of about 60 square miles between Carmichael and the city of Sacramento.

Moore, Craig, and Isenberg were joined primarily by friends and acquaintances who they knew were interested in governmental reform: Fred Boltres, an insurance securities trust fund representative; John Landry, manager of the Crocker-Anglo Bank of Carmichael; Owen Stewart, professor of political science at the American River Junior College (later the executive secretary of the group); and Martin Anderson, a specialist in revenue and finance in the State Controller's office. Anderson invited Eugene Campbell, a highway construction engineer. A building contractor, Win Johnson, and a dentist, Darol Rasmussen, were invited by Stewart. Horace Dunning, one of the first members, became attorney for the committee. All of these individuals had shown interest in or had participated in Carmichael community affairs. Isenberg also called upon Dr. Sam Wood for his expert opinion on the alternatives for governmental reorganization. Wood had been a governmental consultant and a professor of political science for several years and was at this time associated with Pacific Planning and Research, a consulting firm.

Nine of the 14 committee members were interviewed. (An additional 9 persons who favored incorporation but were not on the committee also were interviewed, as well as 2 persons who were opposed.) All claimed to have joined the committee because they were interested in planning, improved community organization, and better services and roads. Each ascribed the same motives for involvement to all 14 members, but some personal factors were also mentioned. The homes of two members had been affected by spot zoning; another member was about to subdivide a fair-sized acreage that he owned, and another member owning property along the main thoroughfare was having difficulty getting new offices built nearby. A proposed new freeway to run near a member's property helped spark his concern. One member allegedly had an interest in becoming planning officer for the new city and one was said to aspire to the position of mayor of the new city. On balance, however, it appears that personal considerations played a surprisingly minor motivational role. The scores of these individuals on the Allport-Vernon-Lindzey Study of Values underline their idealistic bent. The incorporation workers scored higher on the theoretical motivation scale and lower on the economic motivation scale than the leaders in any other movement studied.[3] Other data indicate that they were more highly educated than other leaders studied.

Three main differences of opinion arose among the 14 leaders in the original citizens' committee. The first two were disagreements over goals. Dr. Sam Wood presented the greatest challenge to the Isenberg goal of incorporation. He was invited to join the group a month after the first ten members had organized officially, and at the first three meetings he attended, he strongly supported annexation rather than incorporation. He favored centralized planning for the total metropolitan area. If the city of Sacramento was willing to move "with sympathy" toward annexation, he felt this promised the best solution. The group agreed that statements of city leaders were sympathetic, but not likely to be acted upon. Despite this initial divergence of opinion with the chairman and with the group as a whole, Wood apparently was asked to prepare a feasibility study with his organization, Pacific Planning and Research. The April 14 minutes stated that Sam Wood agreed "to maintain records of the time devoted by his staff and depend upon the future for possible reimbursement."

On April 21, Wood presented a detailed report on the financing and feasibility of the new 165-square-mile city, boundaries for which were set at the April 14 meeting. He reported that the proposed city contained about 80 special service districts. Property tax rates varied from district to district, with the median about $6.81. A municipal tax rate of $4.235 would be needed to provide municipal services to the proposed new city. Sacramento's municipal tax rate was slightly less than $1.50. Wood's report concluded that incorporation of the proposed city was not economically feasible. Incorporation would require an extremely high property tax rate, with county and school district property taxes added to the municipal tax, or a low level of municipal services, or both.

Instead of ending the matter, this negative report from an expert caused the incorporation committee to "come to grips with the facts of life." It agreed that incorporation would provide improved planning, increased coordination of efforts, and more representative government, and even though the new city "would have to move slowly and increase its services as it was possible" the committee should continue to work toward incorporation. Several committee members reported that Wood's enthusiasm for the movement diminished after this time, but he remained a member of the committee and later supported incorporation in radio and television appearances.

Was incorporation a goal in itself or only a means to city-county merger? This second issue was often discussed but never resolved. Those who wanted merger felt that a separately incorporated city would have more leverage to push the city of Sacramento into merger. While the merger element on the committee never publicly gave up its ultimate goal, during the public campaign for incorporation that goal was sometimes dim indeed. Some of the original leaders interviewed still claimed that they were always working toward merger.

The third major difference of opinion was over the type of action program needed to put the new city idea across. Part of the group wanted to conduct a slow educational program. The committee would gradually be increased to about a thousand persons, representing the leadership of all of the organized activities within the proposed city—service clubs, churches, improvement clubs, chambers of commerce. A simultaneous public education program would emphasize the problems in the area and the practicability and desirability of forming a new city. After this educational effort a new citizens' committee was to be formed to set up the machinery to incorporate. The persons who opposed this view are not known by name, but their "crash" or "shock" approach finally won the day, perhaps by circumstance rather than by design.

No one dropped out of the movement because of these differences among the leaders. Some individuals lost their original enthusiasm but this cannot be attributed to Isenberg and Moore, who both worked extremely hard to bring about incorporation.

SMAAC AND MGC MEMBERS PARTICIPATE

Some SMAAC and MGC members played a part in the incorporation movement. A. F. Dredge, Jr., an influential member of SMAAC; James Cowan, chairman of SMAAC and an influential member of MGC; and Elmer Nelson, an Aerojet-General Corporation employee who was a member of SMAAC and for a time of MGC, were all aware of the activities of the incorporation committee well before the public meeting of June 17.

As early as January 30, 1958, when both MGC and, without publicity, the incorporation study group were getting under way, Dredge stated in his first speech as president of the Greater North Area Chamber of Commerce that "if substantial progress is not made in the next weeks we intend to take the lead as the one organization with universal representation in the north area to form a new committee to establish a new city north of the American River."[4] Three incorporation leaders stated that Dredge donated money to their group and was kept informed of its progress from the beginning. He was not officially a member of the group although he was invited to join the committee and later asked to provide names of people to be invited to the first public meeting.

James Cowan, approached for the same two purposes, was

never an active public supporter of incorporation, but by seeking governmental reorganization for the North Area, he gave it his blessing. He told the MGC in June that the incorporation effort must be taken seriously. He listed city-county merger (SMAAC-PAS) as his first choice, mass annexation to Sacramento as his second choice, and the new city as his third choice.

Elmer Nelson of Aerojet-General and John Goodman of Douglas Aircraft were officially approached by Martin Anderson and Howard Craig in the middle of May in order to explain the incorporation committee's plans and to obtain their "cooperative efforts." On May 26 it was reported in the minutes that Nelson and Goodman had expressed interest and appreciation upon being informed of the incorporation movement. City-county merger would be best, Nelson said, but probably could not be achieved. Both men saw the need for governmental change and stabilization of the tax structure and Nelson allegedly offered to help with the incorporation effort. (From later interviews it was learned that Douglas Aircraft had indeed helped, but that Aerojet-General became rather cool to the idea.)

ORGANIZATION

On March 3, when there were but ten members on the committee, Isenberg was elected temporary chairman, Stewart, temporary vice-chairman, and Mildred Welsch, temporary secretary. Mrs. Welsch was from the Arden-Carmichael school district headquarters; she dropped out of the committee in April. Many of the early meetings to study the problem were held at Isenberg's home and he could be credited with bringing the group together and forcing the pace of the original committee. The chairmanship fell to him rather naturally, and the officers were all Isenberg people committed to making the incorporation movement more than a mere foil for forcing the merger of city and county.

As part of the strategy for getting widespread support for the incorporation attempt, the original group of 14 decided that, after the first public meeting, most of them would play a minor public role. One of them was to sit on each of five sub-committees which were to be formed June 17. The remainder were to stay in the background so that it would not look as if Carmichael were running the whole show.

Some of the new members chosen to chair or sit on the new subcommittees were to be chosen prior to the public meeting. The records reveal very little about who was approached and who agreed to serve, but it is doubtful that much was done about developing new leadership before the public meeting. The transition in leadership was awkward and, as it turned out, unsuccessful. Of the 12 persons named to four sub-committees on June 23, four were from the original group and only two of the remaining eight—O. D. Kingsley, an Orange-vale realtor, and Harold Bondeson, the manager of a large shopping center—were later considered to be activists. The executive committee, formed a week later, was composed of Isenberg (chairman), Landry, Dunning, Stewart, Moore, and Yorton of the original group, plus three new people, one of whom never became active, including Alvin W. Meyer of Citrus Heights, and Mrs. Howard Winslow, who was named canvassing chairman.

Kingsley was named finance chairman. Bondeson was expected to obtain the support of the big shopping areas. Alvin Meyer had made the motion to go ahead with the incorporation at the first public meeting. He was put on the executive committee primarily because of his position as president of the

Foothill Farms Improvement Association. He remained with the movement until the end. Mrs. Howard Winslow and her husband, who worked as a team on the gathering of signatures, had never had experience in politics or in canvassing. The leaders viewed both as hard-working, capable workers, but they were never recognized as policy makers. They dropped out after about 60 days of full-time work.

Two other women were also active in the movement, but did not hold official leadership positions. Josephine Brown, the public relations officer for the largest shopping center in the proposed incorporation, Country Club Centre, helped to arrange radio and television programs and to make contacts with the suburban newspapers. She also attempted, unsuccessfully, to get Mr. Blumenfeld, the developer of the Centre, to back the movement. Sign-up booths and loudspeakers were permitted in the Centre to promote signature gathering.

Mrs. Dorothy Orr was probably the most influential of all the newcomers. She was hired as secretary for the movement's office at Country Club Centre. Her immediate superior was Owen Stewart, who was hired as the executive secretary. When Stewart left the post less than a month after assuming it, Mrs. Orr exercised a great many of his responsibilities. She was the only person in the movement who could be reached regularly during business hours, and consequently became the focal point for communications among the leaders and executive committee from the middle of July through October.

In the middle of August several of the early incorporation proponents led a behind-the-scenes effort to oust Isenberg and place another member of the original incorporation group as chairman of the executive committee. The effort did not succeed. As a result, some members of the original group worked to control the incorporation movement and to pep up the lagging spirits of the executive committee and other workers. They were too late, however, and did not act with enough boldness to accomplish their goals.

FINANCES

In the first financial report to the original study committee on May 26, John Landry reported expenses of $186, which the incorporation committee was obligated to pay. Sam Wood's Pacific Planning and Research study probably accounted for $180 of this amount. A total of $5,000 was estimated as the budget for the incorporation effort. One thousand dollars was to be raised by asking each person invited to the first public meeting to pay $10. On June 2, each committee member present donated $5.00 to pay for mailing the public meeting invitations. Evidently nothing further was done to raise money until after the June 17 public meeting. Donations were mentioned at this meeting as the method of financing, but the people present were not solicited as originally planned.

On the twenty-third of June the chairman of the finance committee announced a goal of $5,000, $2,000 of which was to be a bank loan secured by 20 signatures. On July 3 the suburban papers carried a picture of Landry, manager of the Crocker-Anglo Bank of Carmichael, handing a check for $2,000 to the finance chairman.[5] All of the original group and several new committee members and supporters had signed for the loan.

On June 30, a week after the $5,000 budget was approved, a revised budget of $7,580 was adopted to be used for Stewart's salary ($75 per week), a part-time secretary, and rental of a suite in Country Club Centre. The larger budget was adopted in spite of a discouraging response during the first two weeks of public solicitation. One leader said that the original $2,000 gave out rather quickly and that Stewart was not getting paid. By mid-July Stewart stated that unless the incorporation group could get more money the movement would fail. Isenberg reported that they were not going to have the amount originally budgeted because contributions simply were not being made.

What money was raised came principally through the efforts of Jack Moore. The largest donation was $100, and there were several for $25. Few businessmen gave any money. Members of the Greater North Area Chamber of Commerce gave varying amounts as individuals, but not as much as expected. So it went with many of the people approached. One interviewee stated that only one merchant in the Town and Country Village and the Country Club Centre shopping centers contributed. At one point late in the campaign some of the firemen in the Arcade area were reported to have solicited funds door to door, but without much success. About $1,000 of advertising was sold to help finance a flyer for insertion in the *Suburban News-Shopper*.

Services and equipment were donated more readily than funds. Some printing was secured at cost, and an employee of Douglas Aircraft helped get an airplane and cameras for filming conditions in the North Area. The photographs were used at several meetings. One individual donated a mimeograph machine, and minor supplies were donated by a few other people. A local radio station donated a substantial amount of time, and at least one major television program was presented as a public service.

The leaders agreed that less than $3,000 had been spent for the entire effort and that about $1,600 of this had come out of the pockets of the people who had signed the bank note. Finally, everyone agreed that a great deal of money would have been needed to put the incorporation over; estimates ranged from $10,000 to $100,000.

THE DEBUT OF THE NEW CITY PROPOSAL

The incorporation committee, prior to the public meeting, was truly a study group. Some members were convinced from the beginning that incorporation was the only answer, but the group generally discussed issues in a rational, unemotional manner. Several experts were called in to explain procedures for action, and some members personally consulted others who could not be persuaded to speak to the group.

In mid-March, Horace Dunning visited the newly incorporated city of Fremont, California, where he talked with the assistant city manager. At a March meeting John Marshall, senior statistician of the State Board of Equalization, gave estimates of what a new city could expect from the gasoline tax, liquor license fees, and the sales tax. He suggested that they try to persuade the county board of supervisors to permit the city to retain all of the local sales tax collected within its boundaries for the first two years of its existence. About 70 per cent was being allotted to Sacramento County municipalities at that time. On April 7, Lewis Keller, a representative of the League of California Cities, spoke to the group. He explained that the League, which could offer only limited advisory services until after incorporation, favored annexation rather than separate incorporation.

Planning proceeded slowly and carefully until May 26, when the date for the public meeting was set. By contrast, haste and lack of thoughtful planning marked the activities of the last three weeks before the meeting. The committee largely ignored previous advice and policies on organization and procedure. Jack Moore had been designated by the committee to determine the timing of the movement, but if the group was really committed to a slow educational program, he was the wrong man for the job. According to several leaders, he convinced Isenberg that it would be best to spring the plan on the public at an open meeting in the near future.

He and his followers saw too much difficulty and valuable time lost in getting a great many people "educated." The group had the talent and the drive to get the job done. The time was right for swift action—the SMAAC-PAS plan was already dead and MGC seemed to be getting nowhere. Some advocates of moderation evidently were convinced, because a date, June 17, was set for a public meeting. Yet on the very eve of the public meeting the issue was not settled. The virtually unanimous support of the incorporation idea expressed at the meeting of the seventeenth permanently sidetracked the slower approach. The motion from the floor at the public meeting to file the incorporation papers forced the committee to work under the pressure of a deadline. Under California state law a governmental reorganization group has exclusive rights in an area for 90 days after filing a statement of intent to circulate petitions with the county board of supervisors, and the requisite number of signatures must be filed within that period or the exclusive jurisdiction ends.

About 100 persons attended the June 17 meeting. All had received a letter of invitation asking their help in evaluating "a concept for governmental change" developed by "a group of individuals, representing a cross section of the citizens of the North Area." The members of the committee were listed, and Walter Isenberg signed the letter. The plan was presented and explained to the audience and general discussion followed. Jack Moore argued against piecemeal annexation and contended that incorporation would give impetus to city-county merger. (MGC was, in fact, influenced by the incorporation movement to recommend mass annexation of the entire North Area.) "The basic imbalance," he said, "is between Sacramento city and the North Area. Sacramento has shown little interest in sharing their facilities with us. We have to build up our own strength, so that we will no longer be the poor relations they think we are now." A. F. Dredge, Jr., was quoted as saying that there would be "some aroused citizens around the county in the morning." Toward the end of the meeting Alvin Meyer moved to endorse the incorporation plan; it was approved without a dissenting voice. The motion instructed the committee to file with the county board of supervisors the next morning the required materials and documents relative to announcing the group's intention to begin official incorporation proceedings.[6]

The proposal itself was presented in a brief report entitled "Planning for Tomorrow," which was distributed at the June 17 meeting. The report contained a map of the proposed city and criticized the two primary types of government now serving the area. The county government was not organized to supply the many services needed in an urban area, and other services had to be provided by some 90 special districts. This multiplicity of districts was costly and prevented area-wide planning. Other possibilities for governmental change were discussed and declared unsatisfactory.

The new city would have to incorporate as a sixth-class general law municipality, but after a year could adopt its own charter. The traditional advantages of incorporating were listed: one government rendering area-wide services, more self-determination, a more prudent use of land and water, collection by the city of state subventions not now available, more stable financing, and the legal simplicity of incorporation as compared with other governmental changes. One item in the proposal provided that the new city would retain 90 per cent of the local sales tax instead of the 70 per cent usually allowed by the county supervisors. A budget of $4,411,885 was proposed for the first year—a little more than half of the amount estimated by Sam Wood as needed to provide adequate municipal services.

REACTIONS TO THE NEW CITY PROPOSAL

The incoporation plan provoked immediate discussion and interest from many sources within the Sacramento community. The day after the public meeting James Cowan stated that the inaction of city and county officials had "brought this on." "I think it is tragic," he said, "that the City of Sacramento has had so little foresight and has been so concerned with its own tax rate and cost pattern that it would allow this whole north area to grow without showing a willingness to assume some of the cost burden in the area outside the city."

City Manager Cavanaugh replied:

> In the first place the state law is very clear that a city such as Sacramento is prohibited from annexing any area until the people in that area make a formal request to the governing body of the incorporated municipality.
>
> No one in Sacramento's city government has ever stated he would not favor annexation of the area to the north.
>
> The city council never has refused to proceed with any annexation request where comprehensive areas are involved. The council always has welcomed any movement of people in outlying areas for consolidation with the City of Sacramento.[7]

County Executive Tarshes stated that the county government should not get involved, either pro or con. County Supervisor Garlick said that if the people of that area wanted to set up a municipality that was quite all right, but they still would have to pay county taxes. Another county supervisor, Kelley, felt that along with the loss of revenue (from the sales tax) as a result of incorporation the county would also be freed of a lot of problems. City planner Rathfon considered it regrettable that the metropolitan area of the capital city of California should become splintered into numerous city governments. Alvin Landis, chairman of MGC, said that the people of the area had the right to choose whatever governmental arrangements they wished, but that the creation of great numbers of cities, no matter how large, had never solved the problems of a metropolitan region.

On the evening of June 18, five members of the incorporation committee met at the home of Walter Isenberg. They discussed the previous evening's meeting and plans for the future. A news representative from a local television station also taped an interview with Isenberg for use on a news program later that evening. A reporter from the *Sacramento Bee* who was present quoted Isenberg as saying:

> I've never been so busy in my life answering telephones. People I know and people I've never heard of are offering support and asking how they can help.
>
> From every inkling that I've heard I believe we will get widespread support. If we can reach the people I'm certain they will support us.

Neighborhood chambers of commerce in the incorporation areas gave considerable attention and support to the incorporation movement. The Carmichael chamber endorsed the proposed incorporation on the assumption that the SMAAC-PAS proposal had no chance of being adopted. The North Highlands Chamber of Commerce voted 21 to 17 to support incorporation at a public meeting on the question.

The Greater North Area Chamber of Commerce also endorsed the new city movement but not until September 11.

The chamber's Urban Government Committee endorsed the idea, in a 20 to 3 vote, in late August, 1958. A number of the pro voters supported the idea reluctantly, preferring city-county merger. The final vote of approval by the board of directors of the Greater North Area Chamber of Commerce was 18 to 3. Their action had been preceded by a mail poll of chamber members in which 58 per cent of the number responding favored the new city. In any event, only one week remained between the chamber's endorsement and the expiration of the 90-day exclusive period.

Two days after the public meeting, Mayor Azevedo of Sacramento reacted to the proposal by inviting the entire North Area to seek annexation to the city. This, he thought, would be a better solution than separate incorporation, and he was optimistic about the chances of such annexation: "Since I have been on the council, for six years, we have done everything to encourage annexation of areas to Sacramento. We have not turned down a single request and the larger the area the easier it is to provide necessary services because there is a greater tax base." Other councilmen made similar statements, but councilman James McKinney doubted that the North Area favored such annexation and believed that any attempt by Sacramento to initiate it would result in accusations of "trying to swallow up the area." The same evening the Sacramento city council adopted the following resolution: "The council is receptive to annexation of any sizable area contiguous to the city. It is willing to extend the help of the administration and any department of the city."

Isenberg immediately rejected this plan. In a statement the following day, he said:

> It is assumed such interest [annexation of the North Area] is sincere and not the reaction to the earlier filing of a petition to incorporate that great area.

The people of the committee were motivated solely in finding the best governmental system to meet the needs of the residents. We explored all avenues, including annexation. We presented our findings and recommendations to a large group who joined with us in favoring incorporation.

Today, we have no intent to deviate from that path. We are neither qualified nor do we desire to participate in political maneuvering.

We presented and substantiated our findings. It is our firm conviction that the great city we propose should be incorporated. It is our intent to organize immediately to accomplish this purpose.[8]

In later speeches the incorporation leaders charged Sacramento with making an about-face from its long held policy of self-containment, self-satisfaction, lack of interest, and complacency toward the metropolitan area to one of affection, cooperativeness, and willingness to change in the face of a threat to make a separate city. In the spring of 1960, when the leaders were interviewed, most retained their former opinion, that the "city fathers" had no interest in annexing the North Area. They were critical of the city manager, who, they said, lacked vision and feared the addition of a large area would change the political complexion of the city. If the city had a vigorous policy of annexing uninhabited territory, it could have gone out the Roseville Freeway and along both sides of the American River —in effect surrounding the most populous part of the North Area and preparing it for annexation.

In spite of this rejection of its offer, on June 26 the city council instructed the city manager to meet with North Area representatives to discuss questions of annexation, incorporation, and merger. Mayor Azevedo knew of many persons who preferred annexation to incorporation. He pressed the city manager to tell whether or not Sacramento had money available to provide the North Area with municipal services. The city manager replied that it depended upon the size of the area and exactly what services the residents wanted.

The *Sacramento Bee* opposed incorporation while most suburban newspapers strongly supported the movement. The *Bee* pointed out that two of the three reasons announced for separate incorporation no longer applied. The city council was now amenable to annexing the area; and since the proposal had been made public, the council had placed a city charter amendment on the November ballot so that, if annexation were approved, the new areas could have immediate representation on the city council. The amendment also did away with stringent residence requirements for employment with the city government. (The amendment was subsequently adopted.) As for the third reason—that the area would not vote to come in— this, said the *Bee,* was "an arrogant usurpation of the people's right to decide for themselves." The editorial claimed further that the whole incorporation proposal was developed in a series of secret meetings, and that the incorporation group had all of the legal papers ready for filing the very next morning after the proposal was made public—thus making it legally impossible for the residents to choose any other proposal.[9]

Isenberg replied that there was no legal way for the voters to choose between annexation and incorporation in the same election. He stressed that people in this country have the right to meet in private to discuss measures for their common welfare, and may make public statements if and when they please. Isenberg suggested that all keep their tempers and not resort to expressions such as "arrogant usurpations" and "secret meetings."

From the beginning the proposed new city idea received strong support from the *Suburban News-Shopper* and from several suburban newspapers such as the *San Juan Record,* the

Carmichael Westerner, and the *Citrus Heights Bulletin*. On June 26, these three newspapers carried the same editorial, under the title, "Area Incorporation Plan." The incorporation proposal was called a good plan, a workable plan, and one that challenged the imagination. The SMAAC-PAS proposal was best, but the "politicians" had shunted aside the plan of the "experts." MGC was accused of being unfriendly to city-county merger. The editorial writer expressed dislike of Sacramento's "smugness." Under the circumstances, the only feasible plan was separate incorporation. On the same date the *Suburban News-Shopper* carried an editorial under the heading, "Sheer Madness? Oh, Come Now," which defended the incorporation proposal and the 14 persons behind it. All preceding proposals to do anything about the area had been "left to lie there." The residents of the area should consider this proposal carefully and not be concerned particularly with the opinions of the city council of "a town located six miles away on the other side of a river." The *Carmichael Courier* also carried an editorial on June 26 which stated that the charge of "secret meetings" was unfounded. Incorporation had been "planned openly around a framework of the leading citizens of the area."

In a later article the *Courier* praised the incorporation group for its "yeoman service for the people of the Sacramento community" in moving the Sacramento city council to attempt to make the city charter more congenial to annexation. On the same date the *Carmichael Westerner* and the *San Juan Record* accused the *Sacramento Bee* and the Sacramento city council of trying frantically to create a new issue, but the real issue of whether the city and county officials and MGC would stop procrastinating and set up a consolidated government remained.

"Who Killed Cock Robin?" asked the *Citrus Heights Bulletin*. The SMAAC-PAS plan was dead. Why? The officials of Galt, Isleton, Folsom, and North Sacramento deserved part of the blame, but the chief blame belonged to officials of the city and county of Sacramento, who had created MGC to restudy what already had been studied thoroughly over a period of several months.

LAUNCHING THE NEW CITY CAMPAIGN

On the evening of June 23 a meeting was held at the home of Walter Isenberg. Only four members of the original committee were present—Jack Moore, Horace Dunning, Owen Stewart, and Walter Isenberg. Other "incorporation backers" attended, but newspaper accounts mention only three by name: O. D. Kingsley of Orangevale, John Goodman of Douglas Aircraft, and Mervyn A. Neumann, an oil company representative. According to newspaper accounts, the Interim Committee on Incorporation of Greater North-East Area was dissolved at this meeting, and the Citizens' Committee for Incorporation was created.

From early July on, the proponents of incorporation concentrated on selling the idea to the people of the area and getting the signatures of the necessary number of property owners. At a July 1, 1958, meeting at the incorporation group's headquarters at Country Club Centre, a publications committee was created, and it was decided that a series of articles, written by selected individuals but sponsored by the Citizens' Committee for Incorporation, would be printed in the local newspapers over a period of a few weeks. At the end of the series, all of the articles were to be combined into a brochure, to be paid for from the $1,500 budgeted for publicity. Walter Isenberg presided over this meeting, which was attended by five of the original committee and seven or eight others.

Some of the proposed articles were written and subsequently published in several newspapers, but, for lack of funds, the brochure was not printed. The Citizens' Committee for Incorporation sent speakers to community meetings and staged a number of public meetings of its own. Except for two or three of the earlier ones, the newspapers reported very small audiences at these meetings. For the most part, the few meetings called by opponents of incorporation had small attendance also. Generally the public did not seem to see any emergency that called for immediate and drastic action.

Several issues arose concerning signature gathering. The role of the executive secretary, Owen Stewart, in circulating petitions was in question. At least two of the incorporation leaders interviewed felt that Stewart was hired primarily to conduct the canvassing effort. He apparently did spend most of his first two or three weeks doing just that, but he also had to deal with the many other details—publicity, coordination, and organization—of getting the movement under way. All leaders agreed that he was assigned too many jobs to be really effective in any of them. He is reported to have been very discouraged about getting the number of signatures needed. After taking a vacation in the middle of July, he did not return to full-time work. The fact that his tenure as active executive ended within a month after he took over was not widely known.

A second issue involved the number of signatures actually needed to get the incorporation proposal on the ballot. The committee had originally assumed that around 10,000 to 12,000 would be sufficient. Later it was advised that the signatures of both husband and wife were legally required on community property, which meant that a considerably larger number were needed. This was discovered after the canvassing was well along, but still far short of the 10,000 goal.[10] The 24,000 figure was not revealed to the Winslows, who were now conducting the canvassing effort with little help from the executive committee.

About 80 per cent of the citizens approached did sign the petition, but Mrs. Winslow stated that it often took a half hour of explanation and discussion to get each signature. The workers could not get the necessary information from the executive committee to answer citizens' requests for facts or clarification of the leaders' public statements. None of the top people ever talked to the petitioners. Furthermore, the leaders themselves were not helpful in petitioning. One said that, "As an example of the poorness of the planning, one evening the executive board decided that the next day all members would come together and each bring five other people and they would try a saturation petitioning effort in a single area. Of the fifteen people who were each supposed to bring five, only the official petitioner from the area, Mrs. Winslow, and her followers, and Isenberg showed up."

Before long it became apparent that getting the necessary signatures was not going to be a simple task. By early August, community newspapers reported that 300 volunteers were circulating petitions, but that another 200 volunteers were needed. (Fewer than 200 persons ever worked on petitions according to reliable information.)

While the community chambers of commerce generally lined up in support of the proposed new incorporation, the Sacramento City-County Chamber of Commerce went on record in opposition. Its metropolitan development committee had recommended opposition in early July. In early August the executive committee stated that although approximately 40 per cent of its membership was living or working in the area proposed for incorporation, the chamber must place first importance on the welfare of the county as a whole. The Sacramento area could not expect to fare well in the competition between various sections of the state for industrial payroll and tax-producing industries if it did not present a unified approach. Intra-county disputes would harm all of the cities within the metropolitan area in the long run. The Sacramento Area Planning Association also took an official stand in opposition to the incorporation.

Newspaper reports of the public meetings during the summer of 1958 indicate other troublesome issues. Some sparsely populated fringe areas were being forced into the new city; Isenberg stated that after the necessary number of signers had been obtained the county board of supervisors could exclude such areas. Other small communities were concerned about being swallowed up by large city control. Many questions about finance also arose. The people really did not know how much service they would get at what cost, since the proposed budget was merely an estimate on the part of the incorporation backers.

As it became apparent that a special survey under MGC sponsorship might reveal that annexation would cost less than separate incorporation—just as Sam Wood's study had shown earlier—the backers of incorporation began to argue that other advantages justified a possible higher cost. The volunteer fire departments need not be destroyed under the proposed new fire department while annexation to the city of Sacramento would mean no volunteer workers. The job security of the employees of the various special districts would remain unimpaired. (Contrary to this view, the long-range goal of incorporation was the gradual abandonment of all special districts in the new city.) Separate incorporation would allow the residents to determine how their tax dollars were to be spent.

A. F. Dredge, Jr., a supporter of incorporation, was critical of other advocates for proposing an annual budget of only $2,000,000 for roads, when the county currently was spending $4,500,000 annually in the area for roads. Residents were being told that under incorporation they would not have to continue to pay the 25-cent road tax, without being informed that this "saving" would deprive them of $2,500,000 for the construction of streets and roads.

Other possible budget troubles in planning and police protection arose. The county planner stated that the proposed city budget provided only one-third as much for planning as the county already was spending for this purpose in the area. A professor of police science at Sacramento State College estimated law enforcement costs, based upon the expenditures for police departments in cities of about 150,000 population. A complete and fully organized police department for the new city would cost an estimated $1,500,000 annually, but the proposed incorporation budget provided only $800,000 for police. He suggested that it might be cheaper to contract with the county sheriff's office for police services. A month earlier the county board of supervisors had adopted a policy of providing services such as police protection, which the county was staffed to perform, to areas in the county on a contractual basis. (This policy has never been implemented.) No estimate of the contract cost for police services was made, however.

As the above issues and problems became public knowledge, the character of the incorporation meetings changed. At first there had been efforts to analyze what incorporation would mean for the area. Before long, however, a number of the incorporation proponents used the public meetings only to paint the city of Sacramento in unappealing colors. Sacramento maintained a condescending attitude toward the northeast area, annexed only for the tax income the new area would supply, and had a very high crime and tuberculosis rate. On the other hand, the northeast area had one of the highest-type populations in the United States and was willing to contribute time and money to the cause of good government.

EXCLUSIVE CONTROL PERIOD ENDS

The day before the incorporation group's exclusive control was to expire, the county counsel issued a legal opinion that renewal of exclusive control for another 90 days would be illegal. The incorporation group could continue to circulate its petitions, but it no longer would have exclusive control. In fact, another group could file another proposal for part or all of the area and receive 90 days' exclusive control for its proposal.[11] The next day, September 16, 1958, exclusive control was scheduled to expire at 5 p.m. The county counsel stated that if any legal maneuver to extend the period of exclusive control were attempted, the whole incorporation proceeding would be open to court challenge. He said that a petition for a 90-day exclusive period could be filed, but it would be considered a new period. Thus, the backers would have to start all over again to get signatures.

No signed petitions in support of the proposed new city were submitted. While the number of signatures obtained was not announced, failure to turn them in was taken generally to mean that the number was insufficient. In fact, fewer than 8,000 were ever gathered. However, at one minute after midnight of the expiration date, Jack Moore and Darol Rasmussen filed a new petition for incorporation with the clerk of the county board of supervisors at the clerk's home. Walter Isenberg stated that the petitions previously circulated would be withdrawn and held by the incorporation committee. For the time being, the incorporation group accepted the ruling that the exclusive control period was not extended; an entirely new movement was beginning in its place. The incorporation group might take legal action later to reinstate signatures previously obtained, according to Isenberg.

The legality of the second incorporation movement was questioned by the county boundary commission. The incorporation group argued that it did not need to file a map and a legal description of the same boundaries a second time. The county boundary commission refused to act, saying that legal petitions could not be circulated until it had reviewed the boundaries. Meanwhile, the county counsel argued, the second block of 90 days was being spent. Both sides agreed that a court contest might be necessary.[12]

Late in 1958 the city of Folsom posed another legal challenge to the incorporation group. Folsom wanted to annex 800 acres contained within the boundaries of the proposed new city. Isenberg contended that the incorporation group had exclusive rights in the area. The Folsom city attorney contended that the incorporation group had not obtained a second legal 90-day period of exclusive control because it had failed to file the necessary documents. Folsom completed the annexation in 1959, and no legal action was attempted against it.

OPPOSITION FORCES

Backers of the incorporation proposal confirmed in interviews that their most formidable opposition was the *Bee* and city officials of Sacramento. In the preceding narrative of events, the attitudes and positions of these opposition forces have been cited. Two citizen groups and some improvement clubs also presented opposition which, while not causing its failure, did weaken the incorporation movement.

One such group informally organized against incorporation was led by Edwin Morgan, sometime businessman and part-time teacher. On July 7 he made the statement to the press that some people south of the American River were unhappy about the proposed incorporation. He was referring to residents in the area of the proposed city which was designated for industrial development. About 40 per cent of the new city was on the south side of the American River. There was considerable undeveloped land here, and much of this was viewed as prime industrial area by the promoters of the new city. Many people living south of the American River felt they were to put up with increased dirt, noise, and smoke so that the new city could have an adequate economic base for municipal services for the more expensive residential areas on the other side of the river. The people south of the American River generally did not feel that their interests were akin to the interests of the North Area. Morgan himself owned land just to the south of the proposed new city. He stated that at first he only wanted to know why most of the incorporation leaders—the top five, as he put it—were from the Carmichael area, but his actions reflected a personal distrust of the Carmichael community.

Morgan brought together four merchants from the area and five other men. At the first meeting Morgan told them what he knew, and spoke of the "complete change in the area" that incorporation would bring. The group invited Jack Moore and Walter Isenberg to a later meeting and showed them figures they had worked out that varied radically from the estimates in the incorporation proposal. Morgan also approached 12 building contractors who wanted to build subdivisions and consequently were opposed to keeping the undeveloped area strictly industrial. They did not support Morgan's efforts, but later the Associated Home Builders came out against incorporation.

The Morgan group wanted to exclude its area from the proposed incorporation before the proposal went to the voters. The group finally filed protest petitions with 702 signatures of property owners—many fewer than needed to exclude the area. Morgan said that they had about three meetings per week from July 7 until the end of September, when the petitions were filed.

Mrs. Agnes Booe, the editor of a state legislative newsletter, evidently had talked with Morgan and attempted to organize an anti-incorporation campaign of her own. Mrs. Booe stated in an interview later that, as it turned out, she was a one-woman organization:

> I talked to people and they were completely indifferent one way or another. Most were against, but they wouldn't bother to come to a meeting. They asked me to do the work for them. I put out a few circulars on a multigraph, mostly in my own neighborhood. The boy who did the multigraphing also delivered them. The whole operation cost me only a few cents.

Mrs. Booe said that incorporation was not a formidable movement and that it really was not necessary to have anyone against it. If the movement had gotten serious, others would have joined in opposition.

Mrs. Booe's announcement that she was going to organize opposition was made on September 11. About two weeks earlier the Sierra Oaks Vista Improvement Club voted unanimously to seek exclusion of its area from the proposed new city. The Santa Anita Improvement Club, although it never was cited by the newspapers as an organized anti-incorporation group, presented perhaps the most powerful road block to effective action except for the *Bee* and Sacramento city.

Besides overt opposition, the growing interest in the creation of one single large city out of the entire Sacramento urban area presented the challenge of a counterproposal to the incorporation plan. The board of directors of the Sacramento City-County Chamber of Commerce in late September, 1958, voted unanimously in favor of one big city before MGC had presented its proposal to achieve the same end.[13] About ten days later the Associated Home Builders of Sacramento, in going on record in opposition to the proposed new city, came out in favor of one big city for the Sacramento area. The group stated that the incorporation movement was based upon emotion and upon incomplete facts.

THE DEMISE OF THE NEW CITY PROPOSAL

On November 18, 1958, Walter Isenberg announced that the incorporation effort was being abandoned. The task of getting the required number of signatures was too great. About 8,000 of the necessary 22,000 signatures had been obtained. Isenberg asserted that the incorporation group never had claimed that incorporation was the ideal answer, but in view of inaction and lack of interest on the part of county and city officials, it had seemed the best plan available. Isenberg acknowledged that implementing a sound plan for governmental reorganization was the function of MGC, but he charged that the committee had become sidetracked when it limited itself to studying merely annexation versus incorporation.

Earlier Isenberg had written to the four contenders in the November election for the two seats on the county board of supervisors—Fred Barbaria, Jack Mingo, Edgar Sayre, and Walter C. Kelley. Isenberg stated that if his group felt, after the election, that the county board would vigorously encourage and actively help to develop a city-county form of government, the group would endorse and enthusiastically support such a plan. He asked the candidates to answer some questions on the whole problem of government for metropolitan Sacramento. The letter and replies from Mingo and Barbaria were printed in the community newspapers of the northeast area.

The Mingo and Barbaria letters were considered the most satisfactory by incorporation proponents. Mingo favored city-county merger as the ultimate solution, but he would concentrate first on combining the city of Sacramento and the surrounding unincorporated urban territory—essentially the stand later taken by MGC. Barbaria avoided taking a stand on city-county merger, but he felt that the voters should have a chance to decide the issue in the near future. A week earlier he had been quoted in "unqualified opposition" to the proposed new city. The proponents of incorporation either were ignorant of city costs or were deliberately misleading the residents of the area, he said, and favored unification of Sacramento and the surrounding area as the first step toward city-county government. Mingo and Barbaria at this stage had similar views on metropolitan government; both men were subsequently elected. Sayre favored annexation of surrounding areas to the city of Sacramento and did not favor city-county merger. Isenberg said that Kelley "straddles the issue, and fails to come to grips with the fact that an immediate answer must be found."

Isenberg, in giving up the incorporation effort, proposed that the elected officials of the county and the cities publicly acknowledge the need to develop the best plan for governmental reorganization, which could then be submitted to the voters for their decision. The officials should appoint a small group (no more than three) to develop the general framework of the plan, and the group should have about two months to complete this task. A larger group would then review and develop the plan before taking the issue to the voters.

THE INCORPORATION MOVEMENT EVALUATED
BY SELECTED INDIVIDUALS

Isenberg, Moore, Stewart, and Rasmussen were most often mentioned by leaders interviewed as the important decision-makers. Besides these persons, the remaining members of the original committee were mentioned, but as one interviewee said, "This was really a committee at work rather than a centralized organization." (Two of the active people who were added to the original group criticized this "committee system.")

Isenberg and Moore stood out about equally, but well ahead of the others in getting the group to accept their views. Anderson, Dunning, Rasmussen, and Wood evidently had much influence behind the scenes, but made few public statements after the movement got under way. Several of the leaders asserted that the group, as an action group, lacked the ability to proceed with clarity and decisiveness. As one of the petition managers stated, "The underlings did not actually know who the leaders were, or who made the decisions." Dorothy Orr, secretary in the Country Club Centre office from July to October, stated, "They had no machine, and no one even to tell me what to do." They needed an executive secretary to "run things on a professional basis."

In retrospect, the organization for action was poorly conceived, loosely constructed, and largely ineffective. New leadership from the public at large did not materialize and the responsibility for carrying the movement fell to the original planners, few of whom remained fully active. Some, like the Winslows, whose work was vitally important to the success of the movement, were unable to obtain help or decisions in spite of the fact that they were members of the executive committee.

The decision of the original group to play a small public role and support a larger, broadly representative citizens' committee did not work out. The new group could not be instilled with the same fervor and knowledge as the originators of the plan had had, nor could a sufficient number of persons be found to form an effective staff. The idea was abandoned almost immediately. When Owen Stewart was appointed executive secretary, many of the other original members evidently no longer felt a need to work as hard as before. One leader stated, "With a full-time person, many of us relaxed. . . . We should have continued to expend as much effort as we had up to that point." Stewart's resignation left a void that could not be filled with original members. The organization proposed on June 9 remained a paper one; the original group did not develop fully or effectively, and the coordinating and controlling function of the executive committee never worked well. Nevertheless, no leader interviewed was prepared to say that the incorporation movement would have succeeded if the organization had been clearer and more realistic. The primary reason for failure was public apathy, which could have been overcome only under extraordinary circumstances.

The incorporation movement really never got off the ground. The total number of people who were in any way active in the movement did not exceed 200, the majority of whom were individuals interested in governmental change and not members of potentially influential interest groups or organizations in the community.

The only organization mentioned that actively supported incorporation was the Greater North Area Junior Chamber of Commerce, which set up and manned the public address system in the Country Club Centre. A number of leaders of the incorporation attempt reported that some Arcade firemen conducted a house-to-house canvass of several areas for contributions to the movement, but the fire department organization—in contrast to departments involved in other reorganization movements—took no active role. This lack of organizational support was one of the most discouraging factors to the incorporation group. The Greater North Area Chamber did not furnish men and money for the movement, but only passed a resolution in support, after the movement was already doomed to failure. Service clubs such as Rotary, Lions, and Kiwanis were little more than interested audiences to speakers supporting incorporation, and none endorsed or worked for the movement. One leader said that service clubs were inactive because they dislike to endorse issues which may divide their members.

There was no doubt in the minds of the interviewees that the *Sacramento Bee* strongly opposed the incorporation movement. The *Bee*, they felt, wanted to protect "the integrity" of the city of Sacramento and its own political and social influence in the county. It favored annexation to Sacramento because "the *Bee* can get more national advertising if it can show a larger city for its location." The suburban papers, particularly the *Suburban News-Shopper,* published full coverage of all press releases, meetings, and other activities of the movement. The *Shopper* was the most dedicated editorially, while the community newspapers tended to support the movement primarily through attacks on the city and the *Bee*. The realtors located in the area to be incorporated were believed to be in favor of the movement, in contrast to the realtors based in Sacramento. None of the big realty companies gave support, and the Sacramento Home Builders' Association publicly opposed incorporation. According to the interviewees, the big realty companies were opposed because they were exercising major influence on city and county zoning and planning now and did not know what control they could exert on a new city. The downtown Sacramento businesses were said to be opposed because of their vested interests. "There are many empty rooms and stores down there. Taxes are being increased in Sacramento city because of the suburban trend in business." The suburban businesses were reported to have reacted in a manner similar to the realtors. The large businesses and the largest shopping centers would not support the movement, while many of the small independent businesses were said to favor the movement.

Officials of the city of Sacramento were believed by the interviewees to be opposed to the new city. The city, quite naturally, the leaders said, wanted the area left available for annexation at whatever time and in whatever amount Sacramento might desire. The county officials, especially the county executive, were opposed but gave fair treatment and information to annexation supporters. "One thing the county opposed was our idea of giving only 10 per cent of the sales tax back to the county." The county executive "was also disturbed by our accusations against the county government . . . we endangered his empire." Supervisor Kelley was the only supervisor to take a public stand and in the closing days "took a few jabs at us for no reason at all . . . and this might have cost him the supervisorial election." (Kelley was defeated in his bid for re-election.) The incorporation people did not try to force the supervisors into a position on the issue because "in the end they had to approve the petitions."

Several incorporation leaders voiced regret that the League of Women Voters had not endorsed the movement, although they were pleased that many League members worked at securing signatures. The League's official position supported the SMAAC-PAS proposal of city-county merger.

The owners of the big shopping centers and vacant land near Country Club Centre were mentioned most often as individuals who should have been but were not involved. Evidently most leaders originally had held high expectations of support from these people. Aerojet-General Corporation was the only other large business singled out as one which could have aided considerably but did not. Only two individuals were named as persons who should have given stronger support to the movement: Seldon Menefee, a North Area newspaper publisher, and James Cowan, a superintendent of schools and chairman of SMAAC and a member of MGC.

The greatest deficiency in the movement was that its appeal was to small property holders and individual citizens rather than to large businesses and influential interest groups and service clubs. The leaders were sure that some heads of businesses and social organizations would have helped if they had been brought into the planning committee during its early stages. It is significant that if the incorporation initiators had followed their original plans, just such people would have been involved.

The interviewees were questioned about why the incorporation movement failed. Five cited poor planning and lack of organization. Three others stated that it was "lack of money for promotion." Two said that the movement was poorly timed and premature, while four spoke of "apathy of the people" and "lack of enthusiasm for change." A sample of additional responses includes "taxes," "lack of personnel," "did not get enough people involved," and "failure to concentrate on the petitions."

Organizations and individuals did not support the group because they could not see any benefits in incorporation. "We could not provide them with better services, only higher taxes." Many of the residents of the incorporation area, in fact, preferred the capital city to a rival to it, if they must be in a city at all. One interviewee observed: "People who really are concerned on a theoretical basis, such as our group, cannot carry through a movement. There is no strong motive for an arduous campaign. You need some kind of economic incentive in order to get that kind of activity." Most supporters of incorporation concluded that it would take some kind of spectacular or catastrophic event to rally the residents to take any action at all.

CONCLUSIONS

The original idea of Moore and Craig to organize a citizens' group to study the alternatives for governmental improvement appears to have been timely. The SMAAC-PAS report was dead, and MGC, as it developed, had many of the same people on it and seemed at the time to lack a clear sense of direction. As it turned out, the incorporation movement probably helped give MGC a sense of direction, in forcing the committee to face up to and ultimately reject large-scale incorporation as one way of reorganizing metropolitan area government.

Isenberg's strong leadership had an important influence on the movement in all its stages. He worked vigorously on behalf of the committee during its formative stages, and because he took the initiative in calling meetings and in keeping the group active, he became the leader. He was respected and liked in this role, but his devotion to incorporation as an objective in itself seemingly prevented a full review of other alternatives.

Most of the committee believed that in order to achieve success an evolutionary plan of education and recruitment was necessary. Of the original members, at least seven were committed to this method. Examination of the minutes and the interview responses reveals little reason for the precipitous action finally taken by the committee. The decision to take the proposal to the public in a surprise move appears to have ended the careful planning and orderly action that first characterized the movement. The "action organization" was hastily conceived, poorly formed, and never completed. Functions and duties were not clearly delegated; communications and publicity lacked coordination; the organization during the action stage lacked the decisive leadership of the earlier planning stage.

The failure of the movement was virtually predictable. In a sense the opposition had little effect. The people in the North Area have in large part been undisturbed by predictions of future crises in relation to parks, sewers, water, streets, and police. The likelihood of success in incorporating such a large and diversified area would be remote, regardless of the quality of leadership and efficiency of organization.

Several indirect results may possibly be attributed to the incorporation movement. Sacramento County government, recently the subject of much criticism but by then infused with the leadership of a new, vigorous county executive, was revamped further by the unseating of several incumbent county supervisors. Expressions of dissatisfaction with county government that grew out of the incorporation effort added to an already sizable record of criticism and made it easy for the *Bee* and the public to abandon their traditional practice of endorsing the incumbent supervisors for re-election.

The city of Sacramento adopted an annexation policy, explaining that annexations to Sacramento "are encouraged and welcomed" and clarifying the effects on various services after annexation. The city also changed its charter so that residence in annexed areas would count as city residence in meeting requirements for election to city council and for city employment.

Finally, greater general interest in governmental affairs in the North Area seems to have been engendered by the movement. In later annexation elections, voters went to the polls with better awareness of the issues involved. The Hagginwood-Del Paso Heights attempt to annex to Sacramento was conceived when the area was excluded from the proposed incorporation. The Arden-Arcade attempt to annex to the city of Sacramento was begun primarily because a few persons in that area were opposed to incorporation. The new city incorporation attempt highlighted one method of modifying existing government, and incorporation is still discussed on occasion in some of the communities that were included in the proposed big new city.

4

The Hagginwood-Del Paso Heights Annexation Attempt

On July 3, 1958, about two weeks after the incorporation group began its public campaign, the Sacramento city council received a request for permission to circulate petitions for the annexation of certain communities in the county to Sacramento. The areas included were Hagginwood, Robla, Del Paso Heights, Northgate, Gardenland, and most of the McClellan Air Force Base. The area north of Sacramento but south of the American River, not then a part of the city of Sacramento, was also included. The annexation area, approximately 24 square miles, almost surrounded the city of North Sacramento. The new site for the California state fair, which touched on North Sacramento, was not part of the area. A week later permission was granted by the council, and the movement to

annex the area commonly called Hagginwood-Del Paso
Heights got under way.

The immediate impetus for the Hagginwood-Del Paso
Heights annexation request was the attempt to incorporate the
big new city discussed in the preceding chapter. Only part
of the Hagginwood fire and sanitary districts was included in
the incorporation area, but when some residents asked that
all of Hagginwood and some neighboring communities be
made part of the new city, their request was rejected, allegedly
on the ground that boundary changes would cause too much
delay. Several residents of the rejected areas stated bluntly
that the proponents of the new city simply did not want them.[1]
Rebuffed by the new city advocates, the residents of Hagginwood, Del Paso Heights, and neighboring communities looked
to the city of Sacramento. The Sacramento city council had
gone on record only a few days before as being willing to
accept any of the surrounding areas wishing to be annexed.

The question of improving local governmental arrangements
in the Hagginwood and Del Paso Heights communities had
been discussed for several years. In the mid-1950's enough
signatures had been obtained to authorize an election on a
proposal to incorporate Del Paso Heights, but no further action
was taken because of the work of SMAAC. A few months later
spokesmen for the Del Paso Heights Chamber of Commerce
threatened to initiate incorporation proceedings again if North
Sacramento proceeded with the acquisition of the private water
company serving the Del Paso Heights area. In early 1957 the
Del Paso Heights-Robla Chamber of Commerce proposed that
the Del Paso Heights, Robla, and Hagginwood communities
combine to form a new city. Others argued for annexation to
North Sacramento.[2]

The Hagginwood Improvement Association created a fact-
finding committee to study the merits of the alternatives for

governmental reform; their goal was securing municipal-type services for Hagginwood. This committee functioned throughout 1957 and 1958 until the request for annexation to the city of Sacramento was made. The results of a postcard survey, conducted by the committee in 1958, showed that only 23 per cent of the citizens responding favored the *status quo*.

DEMOGRAPHIC SETTING

The population of the Hagginwood-Del Paso Heights annexation area was approximately 35,000.[3] Of this, about 87 per cent was white. The city of Sacramento had the same percentage of white persons; the proposed big city area was 99 per cent white. About 60 per cent of the Negro population of the entire annexation area lived in one area east of North Sacramento.

The population of the Hagginwood-Del Paso Heights area is relatively young. The median age is under 29 years, as compared with a median of over 35 years in most of Sacramento. There is approximately as much rental housing as owner-occupied housing in the annexation area, and about one-fourth of the dwellings were in need of repair. The percentage of owner-occupancy and sound housing is higher in the city of Sacramento than in Hagginwood-Del Paso Heights. This area generally falls lower on the socio-economic scale than do the North Area communities included in the proposed big new city, and there are in fact extensive blighted pockets in it.

LEADERSHIP AND FINANCES

The Hagginwood Improvement Association was a major force for annexation. C. E. Cox, then president of the executive board of the association, and seven other board members signed the original request to circulate petitions. Just how and when the board decided to work for annexation is not clear.

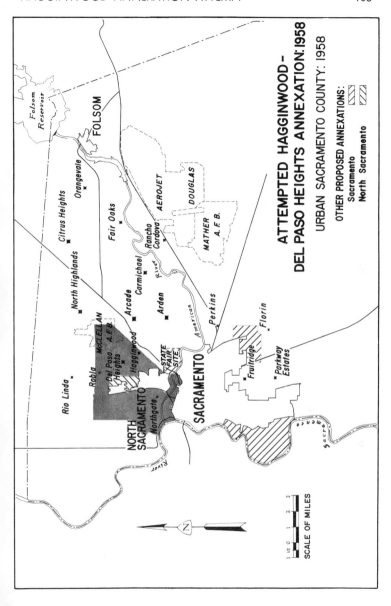

ATTEMPTED HAGGINWOOD –
DEL PASO HEIGHTS ANNEXATION:1958

URBAN SACRAMENTO COUNTY: 1958

OTHER PROPOSED ANNEXATIONS:
Sacramento
North Sacramento

The chief of the Hagginwood Fire District, an active opponent of annexation, stated in an interview that at a meeting of the association a few days after the plan to incorporate the new city was made public, which he attended, the association had decided to ask that Hagginwood be included in the proposed new city. "To my surprise," he said, "one week later I learned that the Hagginwood group had requested the Sacramento city council to grant permission to circulate annexation petitions." It is not clear that any requests to be a part of the new city came from Hagginwood Improvement Association. In fact, two members of the executive board of the association stated that they had attended a meeting of the Del Paso Heights-Robla Chamber of Commerce and had "reversed their [Chamber of Commerce] position in regard to separate incorporation, and in 30 to 45 minutes the potential Hagginwood annexation became the Hagginwood-Del Paso Heights annexation movement."

Of the 10 or 12 persons who led the annexation proposal, all but three came from the Hagginwood Improvement Association's fact-finding committee, or from the association's board of directors, or both. The others included Francis Azevedo, who had attended one of the early public meetings on annexation and had "spoken vigorously" regarding the questionable quality of the schools in the area. He was later asked to become chairman of the publicity committee. Another, John Mogan, was appointed to the executive committee of the annexation committee because of his position as president of the Taxpayers Council of North Sacramento County. E. E. Hodgkinson, secretary of the Sacramento chapter of the Homeowners and Taxpayers Association, Inc., became identified closely with the annexation effort largely because of his frequent pro-annexation letters published by the newspapers.

C. E. Cox and John Mogan were picked out quite early as the leaders. These two divided the total canvass territory between them. Mogan reported that he "got about 24 long-time associates" to circulate petitions and that Cox "lined up" about 20. Newspaper accounts reported recruitment of approximately 100 petition circulators. About 60 of them made some effort, said Cox, but 30 of them "really did it." The active circulators were known as "community workers," and most of them were friends of annexation committee members.

Within this small leadership group there were internal differences. Mogan felt that the directors of the Hagginwood Improvement Association had "jumped the gun" and had made an "unfortunate choice of boundaries." He stated that his group had been waiting for the right moment and that after its premature decision to start the annexation drive the leadership provided by the Hagginwood group was not sufficiently aggressive. These differences of opinion increased significantly during the annexation campaign and the committee membership was revised, excluding anyone from the taxpayers' council. This was not publicized, however, and Mogan, the council's president, continued to support the annexation effort, particularly in letters to the newspapers. He was hard working and dedicated to the annexation idea, but personality conflicts led to the revising of the annexation committee membership.

The annexation proponents who were interviewed were sharply critical of their own leadership. They described it as amateurish and "less than dedicated," but most of them excepted C. E. Cox, whose leadership was considered to be high level but not backed up with adequate support.

An extremely limited budget severely hampered the annexation campaign. Apparently no one kept an exact record, but estimates ranged from $250 to $600. In spite of the city council's policy of active cooperation with annexation groups, it had not yet gotten past the stage of planning how information could be distributed. The work of research and publicity fell entirely on the annexation leaders. Only two or three annexation proponents devoted time to research and "digging up some facts." The publicity chairman assumed the task of "looking up tax bills." Late in the campaign a former newspaper reporter was employed for a period of four weeks at $50 a week to develop a tax breakdown and to prepare a brochure.

THE CAMPAIGN

Despite budget limitations and organizational deficiencies the annexation campaign moved along satisfactorily in the early stages. The Sacramento City Planning Commission recommended approval of the annexation request. The commission reported that the area, which contained about 35,000 inhabitants and had an assessed valuation of approximately $30,000,000, had five fire districts, four sanitary sewer districts, three water districts, three lighting districts, one park district, one flood control district, one high school district, parts of five elementary school districts, and a part of the American River Junior College district. The county boundary commission (with a few minor modifications) approved the proposed boundaries and on July 24 the city council announced approval. After 21 days signature solicitation was permissible.[4]

In mid-July a councilman proposed that the city council promise the people of the annexation area that if they voted favorably for annexation some representative of the area would be appointed to fill an anticipated council vacancy in January, 1959. The council so promised, subject to passage in November of a city charter amendment changing the definition of residency requirements for the city council.

Annexation proponents met on August 11 to plan for the circulation of annexation petitions. Within a month it was reported that 1,200 signatures had been secured. By mid-October about 3,300 signatures, well over the 2,906 signatures required, were registered. The campaign now proceeded to the property owners' protest hearing and, after that, to the election.[5]

The *Sacramento Bee* supported the annexation attempt from the start. The annexation request would test the city's willingness to adopt a "constructively affirmative" attitude toward annexation. The new city incorporation proponents charged that the city of Sacramento was opposed to large-scale annexation. Friendly action on the Hagginwood-Del Paso Heights request could remove all basis for that argument.

During the early weeks of the annexation campaign there was rather minor opposition. The *North Sacramento Journal* editorialized that the annexation area logically belonged with "friendly" North Sacramento and it should not be gobbled up by the "unneighborly big city," Sacramento. The *Journal* urged the affected residents to ask themselves: "Will annexation give me more for less than I can do for myself, or through my local geographical community?"[6] In the first public meetings a number of persons seemed undecided on whether or not to support annexation, but no vigorous opposition was expressed and most of the questions were about the schools in the area. A telephone poll conducted by the *Bee* in the annexation area revealed that about 65 per cent of those responding wanted change of some sort. Quite a few favored city-county merger, but an even greater number favored the proposed annexation.

OPPOSITION FROM THE SCHOOLS

Schools became the major issue in the annexation movement. Up to this time the policy of the city of Sacramento had been to make the schools of the area part of the Sacramento City Unified School District when an area was annexed. Since school merger was not required by law, the question of whether the schools were to be included in the Hagginwood annexation was brought up early in the campaign. Many assumed that the schools would be included, but a number of the annexation leaders stated in interviews that they had understood the reverse; some were quoted in newspaper stories to that effect.[7]

In September, 1958, the superintendent of the Grant Union High School district asked the county counsel for a legal opinion as to whether annexation for municipal governmental purposes must include annexation for school purposes. The counsel ruled that the city could require that the schools in the area annexed become a part of the unified school district, but it need not do so. The decision regarding the schools must be made before the annexation vote.[8] Editorially the *Sacramento Bee* advised the city council that to include the schools as a part of the annexation would invite the superintendents and trustees of the affected districts to spearhead a powerful force against the annexation, which probably would cause its defeat. Leaving out the schools would not prevent a redrawing of school boundaries later.

The city council held a number of meetings on the issue. Representatives of the Sacramento City Unified School District attended some of the meetings and argued for inclusion of the schools. The Sacramento city planner stated that if he had thought that the schools would be included he never would have recommended the annexation. As he put it, the annexation would cut "the guts out of too many school districts." The city councilmen were divided. Finally, on October 23, 1958, the council decided the school issue in a 7 to 2 vote in favor of including the schools in the annexation. The required number of signatures on the annexation petitions had already been secured, and those who signed the petitions had done so without knowing whether the annexation was to include the schools.

Once the decision to include the schools was made, immediate and vigorous opposition to the annexation arose. School superintendents and trustees from the affected school districts organized an anti-annexation group, commonly called the Hagginwood Anti-Annexation Committee or the Citizens' Committee Against Annexation. William L. Frazier, Jr., an employee of McClellan Air Force Base and former trustee of one of the affected school districts, was chairman of the group and public spokesman for it. The "power behind the throne," as seen by some leaders interviewed, was a building inspector in one of the school districts. Other influential members included the president of American River Junior College, three school superintendents, and a fire chief. As one interviewee said, "The organization in a hurry shook down to six or seven persons."

The group soon gave up a plan to block the annexation election through property owners' protests as hopeless. They decided to fight the issue in the annexation election campaign. Even so, the superintendent of one of the school districts secured many of the property owners' protests that were filed. These protests represented only about 5 per cent of the total assessed land valuation; over 50 per cent was required to prevent the election.[9]

The amount of money spent by the annexation opponents and its sources were never known. One interviewee who worked in the movement estimated that about $1,000 had been spent. The County Sheriffs' Association, he said, had contributed from $200 to $300, and he himself had contributed approximately an equal amount. Two or three "community-minded citizens" had been approached for money and had contributed. School suppliers had been asked to contribute and had done so. School teachers had not contributed directly, but "possibly in one or two instances school teachers' associations had earmarked funds in their budgets for this purpose." Another member of the anti-annexation organization, who estimated expenditures of approximately $1,000, claimed that about one-half of the amount was secured from numerous small donors—"teachers and other similarly interested persons"— who gave from $5 to $20 each. The remainder came from business contributions ranging from $50 to $150 each. He spoke of "a contribution from the county sheriff," probably referring to a contribution from the County Sheriffs' Association. A member of the school group reported that all of the $1,000 had come from school personnel, school architects, and school suppliers. He said that the annexation matter had been discussed with school administrative personnel—but not the teachers—and before "passing the hat" they were told that there was a serious likelihood of their losing their employment.

The proponents of annexation guessed that expenditures by the opposition ranged from $3,000 to $15,000. The higher estimates included the cost of a special report and the contributions in staff time by school districts, fire protection districts, and so on. Whatever the exact amount, the anti-annexation forces had more money than they needed. One of the interviewees acknowledged a surplus of funds, and he spoke of the difficulties involved in the effort to return the unused money to contributors on a pro rata basis.

The school issue caused one of the original annexation leaders to withdraw from the movement: "pressure was brought to bear upon me through the schools operating on my son by publicly embarrassing him." Numerous nuisance telephone calls led the father to obtain an unlisted telephone number. Another interviewee alleged that children were sent home with messages pinned to their clothing telling the parents that if the annexation succeeded the children's teacher would be out of a job and that "strange" teachers would be brought in. This was disputed by a teacher in the area who favored the annexation and said that she knew of only one teacher who had done this. Principals made direct collections of contributions for the opposition from teachers, going around to them with a clipboard containing the names of all the teachers and asking how much they wanted to give, another interviewee stated. He added that on the weekend before election "teachers were imported from as far away as Davis and Woodland to distribute anti-annexation literature."

Many of the school administrators of the annexation area were publicly involved in the opposition. It is impossible to tell how much pressure this put on the teachers. One teacher, who had been identified with the annexation movement, refused to be interviewed because of her fear of possible reprisal. However, another teacher, also publicly identified with the annexation movement, denied that there would be reprisals and stated that the reports of school teachers about forced contributions were grossly exaggerated. In her opinion, most of the teachers who contributed money or worked for the opposition did so out of self-interest. She did add that sound trucks owned by one of the school districts "were driven throughout the area on election day propagandizing the voters."

In an interview the school building inspector, acknowledged to have had a great deal of behind-the-scenes control, spoke freely of his part in the anti-annexation campaign. He had stressed the importance of "creating fighting issues" and not simply responding to the charges of the annexation group: "avoid personality involvement in every possible case." He had also opposed having teachers distribute propaganda: "They would need public support for salary increases and other matters at a later time." He summarized his role in the anti-annexation campaign as follows: "I set the stage, conditioned the outcome, and then deliberately kept out of sight."

The school annexation was, however, nearly always at the center of the controversy. Because of the schools the board of directors of the Greater North Area Chamber of Commerce voted unanimously in mid-November to oppose annexation.[10]

Only the public meetings that discussed what annexation would do to the schools drew sizable audiences. The *Sacramento Union* found the "spectacle" of North Area school officials fighting annexation "not enjoyable." As individuals they had the right to favor or to oppose the annexation, but they had no right to plunge the schools into a political fight.

On the insistence of annexation proponents, the city superintendent in mid-November issued a statement on the advantages of school annexation. "Without question" school taxes in the annexation area would be decreased, he said, and he promised reports from the research staff of the city district on how the schools of the annexation area would be administered.[11] The first of a series of three short reports on the school annexation matter was released about a week later. The report predicted a slight increase in the school tax rate within the Sacramento school district if annexation were approved, and a considerable decrease in the school tax rate in the areas to be annexed.[12] (The school tax in these areas was then from $0.61 to $1.45 higher than in the Sacramento school district.) In addition, the report presented policies designed to insure fair treatment for the pupils, the school teachers, other school employees, and the residents of the annexation areas generally.

The second report, released in early December, dealt with school personnel policies. Most of the incoming employees would receive at least comparable pay, and the report set out detailed methods for protecting the job security of both certified and noncertified teachers.[13] The third report, released in early January, 1959, further analyzed the school tax rates. The tax rate for bond interest and retirement, and for state loan repayment, was at least twice as high in the Del Paso Heights, North Sacramento, and Robla school districts as in the Sacramento school district. The North Area school districts would have to pay off their own bond obligations, but they would become full partners in the Sacramento school system without assuming any of the present bond obligations of the Sacramento district.[14]

The Sacramento City-County Chamber of Commerce sponsored a public round-table discussion on the effects of the proposed annexation upon the schools. Representatives of the Sacramento school district, the school districts of the annexation area, the office of county superintendent, and the state department of education were invited to participate. The superintendents of the various affected school districts spoke of the disruptive effects of annexation. Portions of several school districts would be added to the Sacramento school district while other portions would be left outside. Some of the portions not annexed would be left without any school buildings, while others would have too large facilities for the pupils remaining in the districts. All of the school districts other than Sacramento's would suffer a reduction in their property tax base.

The superintendent of the Sacramento school district presented figures to show that school taxes would be reduced by as much as $0.61 to $1.45 per $100 valuation. The president of the American River Junior College acknowledged that school taxes would be reduced, but he argued that the over-all tax burden in the annexation area would be increased. His figures came from the Kimber report.

In late November, 1958, the president of the American River Junior College reported to the college board of trustees that the pending annexation would be to the disadvantage of the junior college and that it would also reduce the effectiveness of the education system in the North Area generally. Upon the president's recommendation, Dr. George Kimber, a professional educator recently retired from the Sacramento Junior (now City) College, was employed to compile data concerning the effects of the proposed annexation upon the American River Junior College.

The Kimber report was released about a month later.[15] In his letter of transmittal, Dr. Kimber stated that his instructions had been to prepare a scientific collection and interpretation of facts without either supporting or opposing the annexation. Nevertheless, his report was unfavorable to annexation. He hoped that the voters, in spite of their understandable interest in city services, would not approve this annexation which would place the unannexed areas in constant uncertainty as to their school programs. Dr. Kimber acknowledged that this annexation would not affect adversely the educational program of the American River Junior College, but he felt it would be followed by other annexations that would have serious consequences for the junior college.

The Kimber report devoted about 50 pages to an analysis of school functions and population and age-group trends in the school districts which would be affected by the annexation. This was followed by a detailed analysis of taxation. School taxes in the annexed area would be reduced, but the total property tax burden would increase, since the cost of other municipal services for the area would exceed the savings in school taxes. The statements and figures presented in the Kimber report were used extensively by the annexation opponents during the final six weeks of the campaign. The report was the basis for the constantly repeated charge that "annexation will bring excessive taxation."

Later analysis of the economic claims made in the annexation campaign pointed out at least three deficiencies or errors in the Kimber analysis.[16] About 33 per cent had been added to the county property tax assessment figures to arrive at the assessed valuation that would be used for city tax purposes. The basis for this was the much higher average in the city of Sacramento property tax assessments than in the county. The assumption might be correct as to the average difference—city assessments ranged from 5 to 60 per cent higher—but the rate was dependent on the nature of the property, and most of the property of the annexation area was more nearly like that with 5 per cent than that with 60 per cent higher evaluation. Secondly, Dr. Kimber used the city tax rate applied to older city areas, which is higher than that applied to the more recently annexed areas. Finally, the report did not bring out the fact that, while most special districts have only the property tax as a revenue source, incorporated areas have access to sales tax and other sources of revenue. Increases in municipal-type services as a result of annexation would not be financed entirely from property taxes.

One of the school superintendents, who himself was actively opposed to the annexation, acknowledged that the author of the report "may unconsciously have lost his objectivity." However one may judge the report, it seems apparent that it had considerable influence on the outcome of this annexation attempt.

FIRE DEPARTMENT OPPOSITION

Four fire protection special districts were largely or wholly within the annexation area. Many members of these favored the *status quo* but did not take any action until the school group provided the leadership. The assistant chief of the American River fire department asserted that the department was neutral in the effort. He personally was involved in a sense, as secretary of the American River Property Owners' Association, which contributed funds to the anti-annexation forces. Practically all of the business and industrial property owners within the fire district were members of the association, but they were not opposed to annexation to the city of Sacramento. They favored annexation of the area immediately north of Sacramento but south of the American River, where property tax assessment evaluations were high. They were not enthusiastic about the Hagginwood-Del Paso Heights annexation as a whole because the proposal included areas in which slum conditions prevailed. They feared that areas of high assessment evaluations would be taxed inequitably to bring up the level of services in the poorer areas. (The Hagginwood-Del Paso Heights annexation area was excluded from the proposed new city for the same reason.)

The Natomas fire department actively fought the annexation through the Natomas Fire Association. Interviewees reported that the fire fighters prepared anti-annexation literature relating primarily to fire protection matters. Each association member was made responsible for a portion of the Natomas district; every household in the district was to be approached. The firemen distributed their own material and that of others from house to house. They claimed that they opposed annexation not as firemen but as public-spirited citizens.

The chief of the Del Paso-Robla fire department at the time of the annexation attempt said that he had worked actively against annexation. He stated that three of the four full-time members of the department and six or seven volunteers also had worked against it. Some of them worked under the direction of the Hagginwood Anti-annexation Committee as block captains, responsible for the distribution of anti-annexation material. The group tried to convert pro-annexation individuals through a follow-up visit or telephone call by a member of the anti-annexation committee.

The chief of the Hagginwood fire department said that he had taken only a small part in anti-annexation activities. He had appeared on a television program and had talked against annexation to persons in his neighborhood. No other member of his department took part at all, he said. One of the leaders of the Hagginwood Anti-annexation Committee attributed greater activity to this fire chief. The chief, he said, had attended the first anti-annexation meeting, had joined the anti-annexation committee, and had helped prepare anti-annexation literature. Hagginwood firemen had conducted a door-to-door anti-annexation campaign, according to this interviewee.

Although the effect of the opposition of fire department personnel cannot be measured, they certainly provided the mechanism for house-to-house coverage. The fire chiefs viewed the effectiveness of the school administrators as minimal and maximized their own activities as contributing to the defeat of annexation. One fire chief spoke of the strategy of the school administrators as ill-advised and in some instances improper. In his opinion, "All you have to do is talk with people, secure their trust, and enlighten them as to where their interests lie. If enough of this is done, you can win any campaign."

The school administrators in turn tended to downgrade the effectiveness of the fire departments in fighting annexation and to view their own efforts as crucial to the defeat of annexation. In substance, they felt that the fire departments' activities "were of some help, but unorganized. They did assist in the last-minute pamphlet distribution, and they were cooperative and they deferred to our group for leadership."

Two of the annexation proponents, who were long-time residents of the area, believed that the fire fighters' work had a great effect on the outcome. Between 60 to 80 volunteer fire fighters and members of their families had participated. They were interested in preserving the "neighborhood club" atmosphere of the fire stations. "There are pool tables, cards, friends at any hour of the day or night. If the service is professionalized, this home away from home would be destroyed."

OTHER OPPOSITION

At least three of the major annexation supporters spoke of opposition from members of the county sheriff's department, which, they said, believed that "annexation would affect adversely the number of employees required to staff the department." However, no direct evidence of such opposition was presented. Other annexation leaders insisted that county officials and employees worked indirectly against annexation, but presented no proof of such activity.

Pro-annexation interviewees identified activities of other groups to protect their job interests: employees of a sanitary district, bus drivers of a private transportation company, and the building trades people of North Sacramento. It was alleged that the latter hoped for annexation of the area by North Sacramento. No substantial evidence of overt activity against the annexation proposal from these groups was given.

McClellan Air Force Base, which was almost entirely within the annexation area, did not take an official position, but some annexation proponents felt the base had taken a position on the issue. Some annexation and some anti-annexation leaders were employed at the establishment. Base officials followed the annexation battle closely but impartially since Air Force property was potentially affected.

LAST-MINUTE CAMPAIGNING

On January 16, 1959, four days before the election, the *Bee* printed a prediction by annexation leader C. E. Cox that the opposition would level a "sneak punch" against annexation. The *Bee* editorial deplored this type of tactic and urged that informed voters firmly reject "the obvious assumption of the late release that the people can be made patsies, dupes and fall guys." The next day, Friday preceding the Tuesday election, some anti-annexation material was distributed door to door. Parents in the annexation area also received through the mail a mimeographed letter, under the school district letterhead, signed by the superintendent of one of the affected school districts. A postscript stated that the cost of preparing and mailing the letter had not been paid from school district funds. Parents were urged to oppose disruption of the school system. One supporter of annexation, although not a member of any official group, described this "avalanche of confusing and contradictory material" as evidence of "an ulterior motive" behind the anti-annexation campaign. The material was credited to the Citizens' Committee against Annexation.

One leaflet on pupil transportation compared in pictures and words the school buses of the North Area districts with the public transit buses used to transport city school children. The leaflet stressed the special safety precautions taken on school buses and claimed that school bus transportation was free while the public transit buses charged about $45 per pupil per school year. This leaflet also announced a half-hour local television program on annexation scheduled for Saturday afternoon preceding the Tuesday election. The people would learn that annexation meant two tax bills (city and county) instead of one. The other leaflet, "Who's Distorting the Facts?" showed that the city assessed valuation of a few major commercial properties was higher than the county assessed valuation of such property, but no mention was made of the tax rates applied by the city and county on this assessed valuation.

The 16-page pamphlet, "What Does the Hagginwood-Del Paso Heights Annexation Mean to You?," covered a wide range of material. At one point, a property owner in recently annexed Meadowview was quoted as saying that instead of the promised tax reduction his taxes were $211.86 more than in the year preceding the annexation. The pamphlet presented the Kimber report predictions of higher taxes and asserted that property owners could get street lights, curbs, and sidewalks only if they were willing to pay for them. The impact of annexation upon the North Area school districts and upon police and fire protection was also stressed.

Officials of the city of Sacramento immediately declared that they had not promised a tax reduction but only that the services needed in the area would be provided at less cost by the city of Sacramento. As to the higher tax bill in Meadowview, the officials pointed out that regardless of annexation the county tax had increased; that during the first year after annexation the bill contained an assessment for a sewer system installed before annexation; and that the county tax bill would have been even higher if it had included special districts' taxes, which were eliminated after annexation.

The Citizens' Committee against Annexation also ran an ad in the *North Sacramento Journal* headed "Don't Be Fooled." A shark was pictured gobbling up a fish labeled "Hagginwood, Del Paso Heights, Gardenland, Arden, Arcade, and Industrial Park." There were references to Kimber's predictions as to tax increases and to the effects upon the North Area schools. In addition to such printed propaganda, one school superintendent called a meeting of about 170 school principals and teachers and presented his views of the annexation to them.

Probably because of limited financial resources, the annexation advocates prepared and distributed only one piece of printed material, a document of four pages. It urged a "yes" vote to making the area a part of "the heart of California." Fourteen points in favor of annexation were listed, followed by a discussion of alleged benefits which annexation would bring to the educational system. Substantial reductions in the total property tax burden were promised for most of the annexation area. This pro-annexation material did not receive the widespread distribution which the anti-annexation material did.

THE VOTERS DECIDE

The day of election arrived—January 20, 1959. Sixty-nine per cent of the voters registered voted. The annexation was defeated by 159 votes. (This did not include 25 absentee ballots, but these could not affect the result.) The annexation proposal fared worst in the Gardenland area immediately west of North Sacramento and in the area south of the American River, where the issue lost by a margin of about 2½ to 1. In the Ben Ali area to the southeast of Hagginwood the issue lost by a 2 to 1 margin. In the northern portion of the Northgate area the issue lost by somewhat less than 2 to 1. In all other areas where annexation was rejected the margin of defeat was slim.

Annexation won in only five of the 16 precincts. Four of these precincts were contiguous and comprised the eastern three-fifths of Del Paso Heights, bordering McClellan Air Force Base on the southwest. The other precinct where annexation was favored was in the southern portion of the Northgate community.

In restrospect, William Frazier, an active anti-annexation leader, stated that it was the school issue that had defeated annexation. The people did not vote against the city of Sacramento but rather against this unplanned (as far as schools were concerned) annexation proposal. C. E. Cox, one of the pro-annexation leaders, said somewhat bitterly, "It was beaten by employees of the voters, at the voters' expense in some instances, with a direct appeal to ignorance at the last minute." His comment implied that the school officials spent taxpayers' money to fight the annexation proposal.

The school superintendents in the annexation area were spurred by the defeat to attempt to unify the school districts. Unification had been defeated by the voters on December 3, 1957, and at that time the school superintendents had not been enthusiastic about unification. One school superintendent stated that he had changed his mind about unification; it now seemed necessary if the schools were to be kept out of local politics.[17]

Sacramento's mayor, Clarence Azevedo, believed that a second attempt to annex the Hagginwood area would succeed. He noted a number of other instances (Elder Creek and Riverside, for example) in which a second attempt at annexation had succeeded. Annexation proponents would be ready a second time to counter the misinformation given right before the election.[18]

Some of the interviewees expressed surprise that annexation received strongest support in the poorer areas of Del Paso Heights. They had expected opposition from these residents because of their presumed fear that the city of Sacramento would compel them to spend money to improve their housing. Apparently they felt that taxes from the areas of higher assessed evaluation would be used to improve conditions and services in the poorer areas.

HAGGINWOOD-DEL PASO HEIGHTS ANNEXATION EVALUATED BY PARTICIPANTS

Fourteen persons were interviewed in connection with our study of this annexation attempt. Seven had been opposed to the annexation, six had been in favor, and one stated that he was completely neutral.

Annexation opponents agreed that the *Sacramento Bee* was an extremely potent force for annexation, while proponents considered the *Bee* to have been "responsible" but "passive" in the campaign. The *Bee*'s motives were variously appraised by anti-annexation leaders: the *Bee* became involved in order to prevent the emergence of a strong newspaper; the *Bee* was a crusader paper—"a bigger Sacramento is a better Sacramento."

The attitudes of school officials were summarized well by one annexation proponent:

> Unfavorable . . . school officials felt two things: first, that their school district boundaries were being violated in an unfortunate manner and that areas would be left out of

the Sacramento Unified School District; and secondly,
that their own status would be adversely affected if they
became part of the city school system in the sense that
they would be subordinate to a new layer of officials up
above them.

An annexation opponent agreed generally, but added that
"there was a genuine conviction that the area proposed for
annexation would ruin the tax base necessary for effective
school operation in those adjacent areas not annexed."

Few of the activists interviewed believed that the downtown
businesses in Sacramento had been at all concerned, although
businesses were hopeful for the broader tax base and expansion of the city that annexation would bring. Most suburban
businessmen favored annexation, according to the annexation
group, but were unwilling to state so publicly for fear of
offending some customers. Annexation opponents asserted that
suburban businesses had not taken stands on the matter but
that some individuals had favored one side or the other.

With only one exception, leaders on both sides of the movement who were interviewed believed that city officials had
strongly supported the annexation. Proponents felt that the
city had several motives for favoring annexation. Sacramento
did not want a number of small and inefficient neighboring
cities to develop. One said, "Since the entire metropolitan area
is called Sacramento, city officials quite properly are concerned about improving conditions in any blighted areas that
might exist in the metropolitan area," and since the area in
question contained at least one commonly acknowledged
blighted region, the city was properly worried. One annexation
leader said that city officials thought that a larger city would
increase their political influence. Anti-annexation leaders gave
only one reason for the support by city officials: city officials—
and government officials everywhere—believe that "bigger is
better."

Most leaders believed that county officials had opposed the annexation out of fear that county responsibilities and size of operation would be reduced. County officials resented the *Bee*'s criticism of the county sheriff's office, and although these officials had not publicly opposed the annexation, they had supplied indirect help and encouragement to the anti-annexation forces.

All interviewees were asked, "If you were to attempt such a movement again, what changes would you make?" The annexation advocates had numerous suggestions. There was general agreement that the school issue should be kept out of a second annexation attempt. As one of them said, we must find a way to "tie the hands of the school people." Leaders emphasized the need for more money. A publicity man should have been hired early in the campaign. Some felt they should have sought out persons who had time to give to lead the movement, and involved many more organizations and groups. And finally, they came back to a way of dealing effectively with the opposition and preventing "the servants of the public from acting against the best interests of the people whom presumably they are serving."

The Hagginwood-Del Paso Heights annexation movement differed from others studied in that the public could see immediate, specific advantages from joining with the city. The area had a low level of municipal-type services, and it also had a comparatively low assessed valuation. By unification with the city of Sacramento, the city's greater tax resources could be used to help build up the level of governmental services in the annexation area. Perhaps for this reason the Hagginwood-Del Paso Heights annexation came closer to succeeding than any of the other reorganization efforts studied. (Nearly all of this area is a part of Sacramento city today.)

5

The Arden-Arcade
Annexation Attempt

On November 18, 1958, the attempt to incorporate a big new city northeast of Sacramento was officially abandoned. Almost immediately thereafter a proposal was made for the city of Sacramento to annex the Arden-Arcade area. The area encompassed about 24.5 square miles, with an estimated population of 73,000 and an assessed property valuation of about $17,600,000. The Hagginwood-Del Paso Heights annexation was approximately the same size but included only one-half the number of residents. Both the Hagginwood-Del Paso Heights plan, which was nearing its election date of January 20, 1959, and the Arden-Arcade effort were on a much larger scale than any annexation previously attempted. The Oak Park and Eastern Sacramento annexation of 1911, which added 9.4 square miles and approximately 12,000 people to a city of 54,000, was the largest annexation to date. We should also keep in mind that during the period of the Hagginwood and Arden-Arcade annexation movements the Metropolitan Government Committee was seeking to develop a plan of government for the entire metropolitan area.

Although the Hagginwood-Del Paso Heights annexation effort presented an immediate precedent, and MGC was subsequently to propose large-scale annexation, the "new city" incorporation proposal actually triggered the Arden-Arcade annexation movement. From one perspective, the already existing annexation sentiment was organized into a counter-movement to incorporation. A group of citizens who had been considering annexation joined together informally, not publicly, to oppose incorporation. The same people later formed the annexation committee.

The earlier proposals to annex were known to many Arden-Arcade citizens, and the activities of SMAAC and MGC had kept the issue of metropolitan governmental reform alive. In addition, a core of leaders had formed, prior to 1958, primarily around efforts to improve services for local communities in the northeast area. Yet the fact that the catalyst for annexation was anti-incorporation, rather than pro-annexation sentiment had implications for the leadership structure and the history of the movement. Reformist leaders with similar long-range goals found themselves opposing each other rather than banding together to try to overcome the general apathy among the residents of the area. In addition, the timing and the strategy were based on reaction rather than on carefully developed planning. In summary, the Arden-Arcade annexation movement was fostered by negative reaction to the incorporation movement; the impractical proposals of SMAAC-PAS, and MGC's inaction; and a reservoir of experienced community leaders, who wished to avoid the multiplication of special districts and to improve government in Arden-Arcade.

DEMOGRAPHIC SETTING

The nine census tracts which compose the Arden-Arcade district, and which approximate the boundaries of the annexation area, had a population of 73,352 in 1960, making it one of the ten largest unincorporated districts in the United States.[1] It is, of course, not an official district at all but a group of subdivisions relying upon special districts for municipal services. However, in news releases from the United States Census Bureau, it sometimes is referred to as an unincorporated district. Ninety-nine per cent of the persons in Arden-Arcade were classified as white; in the city of Sacramento only 87 per cent are white. The population of Arden-Arcade is comparatively young. The median age does not exceed 35 years in any area and the median is under 30 years in most areas. In comparison, the age of citizens in the city of Sacramento varies much more widely. Slum housing is not a problem in Arden-Arcade. Well over half of the houses in the area are owner-occupied and over 90 per cent of all the dwellings are in sound condition.

In summary, the Arden-Arcade area is a middle-class, white, residential suburb; the population density is rather low, although few expanses of unimproved land still exist. Most of the homes are single-family dwellings occupied by the owners, with long-term mortgages. Since there is little industrial employment in the area and the commercial activity is primarily retail merchandising, most of the working residents commute to the city, to McClellan Air Force Base to the north, or to Aerojet-General Corporation and Mather Air Force Base to the southeast. Many state government workers, who have offices in the city, reside in Arden-Arcade.

Although the commuters put a strain on roadways, there is less traffic congestion in Arden-Arcade than in the city. The police force is limited to officers provided by the county sheriff's office and the California Highway Patrol, but the crime

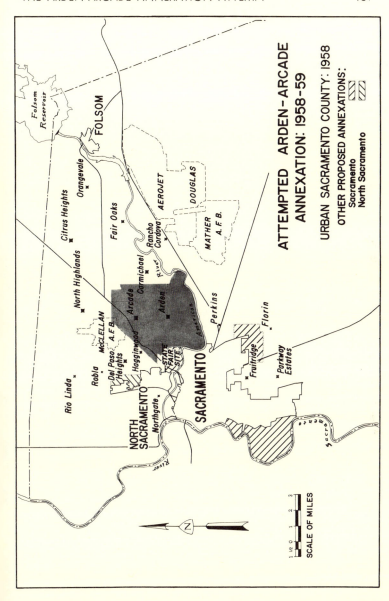

ATTEMPTED ARDEN-ARCADE
ANNEXATION: 1958-59

URBAN SACRAMENTO COUNTY: 1958

OTHER PROPOSED ANNEXATIONS:
Sacramento
North Sacramento

SCALE OF MILES

rate is low. The inefficiency of the numerous special districts in supplying water, fire protection, and other services is criticized but has caused no serious difficulties. A suburban area with no slums, no serious traffic problems, and reasonably adequate services is likely to resist efforts to merge with the central city.

LEADERSHIP

The original impetus and the leadership for the annexation movement came from the Santa Anita Improvement Club, which represented about 1,500 residents. The club had promoted installation of street lighting and establishment of a park district for its area, and difficulties encountered in achieving these goals provoked discussion of the idea of annexation to the city of Sacramento. These citizens knew of the developments in SMAAC, and were aware of the PAS report and the work of MGC. Discussions between the club president, Frank Stipak, a civil engineer for the United States Bureau of Reclamation, and former president E. A. Pesonen, a conservationist for the same agency, led to the first overt efforts toward governmental change. Stipak and Pesonen began to get in touch with friends and other individuals active in civic clubs in the summer of 1958 in order to locate and assess the anti-incorporation sentiment. Stipak was later to become co-chairman, and Pesonen treasurer, of the annexation group. One person involved in annexation suggested that the notion of annexation had been born much before this. Several years earlier many citizens had worked to get a water district for the area. Some of the leaders in this movement later became active supporters of annexation. In addition, many residents who had moved to Arden-Arcade under the assumption that the area would soon become a part of the city were becoming impatient.

Besides Stipak and Pesonen, other leaders of the annexation group included Stanley Kronick, formerly an attorney for the United States Bureau of Reclamation and in private practice in the city at the time of the movement. He was an early member of the group and became co-chairman. His wife had been active in Democratic Party work in Sacramento County. Frank Bragg, another ex-president of the improvement club and then an employee of the California Department of Fish and Game; Wardon H. Moul, the Special Districts Supervisor of the County Department of Public Works; and Mrs. Doris Murray, who was active in women's affairs and the Democratic Party, complete the list of initial leaders for annexation. The core of leadership remained small throughout the course of the movement.

Why did the participants become active? Why did these citizens give so freely of their own time and in many cases, apparently, of their own money to seek to modify the metropolitan governmental structure? From interviews with 11 of the pro-annexation leaders (9 anti-annexation leaders also were interviewed) we get a partial answer to these questions. No campaign promises were made to those who became leaders. They were not offered positions or special benefits of any kind. Rather, the active participants were imbued with a genuine interest in civic improvement. They felt they ought to stop talking and do something about community problems. One respondent pointed out clear difficulties in zoning, parks and recreational needs, and sewer systems. He said that the Santa Anita Improvement Club had discussed the recommendations of SMAAC and MGC and had decided that annexation was a more practical and immediate answer to the needs of their area. Another interviewee felt that annexation was the natural solution to their problems: "there was a general realization that this rapidly urbanizing area needed a less haphazard form of government. The city already existed with an integrated structure for an urbanized area. Therefore, it follows that the city boundaries should be extended."

This respondent, turned theorist, suggested one reason for the failure of the movement: he thought that the leaders were "visionaries" who foresaw that the cost of government services under the existing multiple-district setup would continually increase. This type of person is in the minority, he said, and most people could dedicate themselves only to objectives more tangible than long-range good government. The leaders anticipated problems—taxation difficulties, road and sanitation inadequacies, recreational deficiencies. Immediate, urgent problems were not identified, nor were they manufactured to gain support for the campaign.

Pro-annexation leaders agreed that Stipak, Pesonen, and Kronick were the central leaders throughout the movement. One interviewee gave Stipak the label of "Mr. Annexation," and stated that he had done "more to arouse interest in something that would contribute to the community than anyone else." Kronick, a lawyer, was pushed before the public most often, one interviewee said, partly because the other annexation workers were not widely known and partly because most of them, as government employees, were afraid to be too much in the public view.

THE ANNEXATION MOVEMENT TAKES FORM

The Arden-Arcade District Council of Improvement Clubs, of which the Santa Anita club undoubtedly was among the most active, initiated the annexation effort. Seeking to stall the new city incorporation effort—or anticipating that the incorporation effort might fail—a few members of the council began to speak out in public for annexation of the Arden-Arcade area to Sacramento in July, 1958. The Santa Anita club adopted an official resolution requesting the city to make a study of suitable boundaries for an annexation proposal that would include Santa Anita. E. A. Pesonen went before the Sacramento city council on September 17 with the resolution. "We are now represented by a rash of districts," he said, and he asked the city's assistance in promoting annexation.[2] The council agreed to supply the information but emphasized that its intention was not to "harpoon the proposed new city." Approximately two weeks later the city manager and the city planning director were instructed to meet with the club members.

The evening before the incorporation effort was officially abandoned, the Arden-Arcade District Council of Improvement Clubs voted unanimously to call a public meeting to determine whether there was enough interest in annexing to Sacramento to justify further exploration. About 65 persons attended the meeting, which was held on December 18. The group was overwhelmingly in favor of getting annexation under way. Thirty-nine persons signed a petition to request annexation. The petition was rushed downtown, since the city council was meeting that same evening. The council accepted the petition for filing. The proposal was referred to the city planning commission for study and a report, and Sacramento's mayor promised that the city staffs would assist the annexation proponents in gathering data.

The annexation group was not formally organized until after the public meeting in December. In fact, according to Stipak, the organization did not crystallize until March, 1959. Stipak himself worked mainly with the mechanics of getting the movement started. The organization, as it finally emerged, was called the Arden-Arcade Annexation Committee and had four committees—research, publicity, precinct organization, and finance. Stanley Kronick and Frank Stipak were co-chairmen of the group, and E. A. Pesonen was treasurer. Kronick, William Carah (an employee of the California Water Commission and chairman of the publicity committee), Pesonen, David Yorton (a local attorney in private practice and chairman of the Arden-Arcade council), Stipak, and Mrs. Murray seem to have been the early planners of the annexation campaign. J. R. Liske, an architect and Santa Anita resident, later joined the leadership, representing the city-county chamber of commerce, which had offered its support for annexation. This group developed a two-phase approach—supplying the facts and disseminating these facts as live news. Members of the research committee were chosen as experts in taxation, governmental structure, and other technical fields, and not necessarily because of their support of annexation.

The group made an effort to reach the uncommitted, who would not normally attend public meetings but who might respond to speeches before their civic clubs and other organizations. Most of these talks were given by Stipak, Pesonen, and Kronick. Mrs. Murray tackled the second immediate problem, that of getting the necessary signed petitions in support of annexation. The leadership, structure, and purposes of the movement were easily established, probably because most of these people had worked together earlier and knew each other's interests and abilities. Some of the annexation committee members, however, did not participate at all or contributed very little.

While the annexation question was not a political party matter, charges of partisanship were made occasionally. Partisanship entered primarily because some of the annexation leaders happened also to be leaders in the Democratic Party organization in the area and found it convenient to use the party machinery and the registration lists. Measured by voter registration and by election results, the area is predominantly a Democratic Party area—as is generally true of metropolitan Sacramento as a whole.

On January 26, 1959 (the Hagginwood-Del Paso Heights annexation had been defeated on January 20), Sacramento's city planner announced that he would recommend approval by the city planning commission of the proposed Arden-Arcade annexation, with the schools excluded. The planning commission voted approval of the annexation, but referred the question of the schools to the city council since the commission members felt that they had insufficient information. The annexation proponents, when filing their petition, had suggested that the schools not be involved unless the forthcoming referendum to create the San Juan Unified School District was rejected. The city council, on February 6, agreed to this and waited until after the March 24 election to decide about the schools in the area. The school consolidation referendum was approved and the schools did not become involved in annexation.[3] The county boundary commission approved the boundaries on February 20, with the recommendation that a bordering commercial area, Arden Fair, be included. The suggestion was not accepted.

In early April, Sacramento's city council announced that the various legal requirements preceding the circulation of petitions had been met and that the effort to secure legal signatures could begin on April 18, 1959. It was definite by this time that the schools were not to be included.[4] In the meantime, Mrs. Murray had recruited a corps of petition circulators, primarily from those with whom she had worked as Democratic precinct worker. Between 200 and 300 persons signed up to solicit signatures, but many of these collected few if any signatures. Some individuals, when interviewed later about the movement, took it for granted that she used the Democratic

Party precinct worker cards, but did not involve the party as such.

During the four or five days immediately preceding the beginning of the drive to secure signatures, there was a house-to-house distribution by volunteer help of the newspaper tabloid, "Progress News: Arden-Arcade Annexation." The tabloid announced the opening of the campaign to secure signatures, and listed the qualifications required of the signers. It emphasized that the schools were not affected and that the Sacramento City-County Chamber of Commerce and MGC had endorsed the annexation proposal. Existing conditions within the annexation area were described as a "study in frustration." Included was a table of annual costs of operating a $15,000 home in the area compared with equivalent costs in the city of Sacramento. In one district the cost would be the same. In four districts the annual cost would be from $5 to $19 less, and in the remaining two, which had no sewers, the cost would be $7 more annually. Sacramento's new annexation policy was summarized. Finally, the tabloid included an appeal for funds.

At a public meeting, called for April 15 to explain how the signatures were to be obtained, Mrs. Murray reminded workers that "signing the petition does not obligate the resident in any way. It does not mean he has made up his mind how he'll vote. It merely makes it possible for us all to vote."[5] The canvassers received the registered voters list for the precincts, and only persons listed as registered voters were to be asked to sign. Invalid signatures were thus kept to a minimum. In addition to the precinct effort, booths were set up at some of the shopping centers in the area to collect signatures.

Petition circulation went surprisingly well; about 3,500 signatures were obtained during the first six days of the drive. In less than a month, signatures in excess of the total required had been obtained. On June 15 (the day of the last meeting of MGC), the county clerk certified that there were more than enough signatures on the annexation petitions.[6]

OPPOSITION EMERGES

On April 29, early in the drive to obtain signatures for the annexation petition, Benjamin Frantz announced the formation of the Arden-Arcade Preservation Committee—with himself as chairman. At that time he was also secretary of the Sierra Oaks Vista Improvement Club, which had gone on record as opposing the annexation. The preservation committee was committed to maintaining the local identity of Arden-Arcade, to protecting the suburban way of life, to collecting data relative to any and all governmental reorganization proposals affecting the area, and to assuring local representation in taxation matters. A week later the name of the opposition organization was changed to the Arden-Arcade Government Committee, with headquarters in the law offices of J. H. Tredinnick. It was the only formally organized opposition group throughout the annexation campaign.

The committee listed four major objections to annexation. Annexation would increase taxes. It would hinder achievement of city-county merger because the city of Sacramento opposes this solution to metropolitan problems. The large city would not take time from its own problems to consider those of Arden-Arcade. And finally, the group stated that the area would not be represented on the city council for five years; this last statement was almost immediately retracted.[7]

Benjamin Frantz announced that his group would seek to obtain signatures from over 50 per cent of the property owners in order legally to prevent the holding of an annexation election. He said that 20,000 protest forms had been printed and that approximately 100 persons had volunteered to conduct a door-to-door campaign for protest signatures.

Approximately 1,150 protest signatures had been filed by July 23, the date set by the city council for the property owners' protest hearing. A week later the council announced that the protests that had been filed represented only about 9 per cent of the total assessed land valuation of $17,566,600. The protest hearing was declared officially ended, but annexation opponents were authorized to file additional protests up to the close of the business day on August 10. By final tabulation only about 18 per cent of the total assessed land valuation was represented by the protest petition signatures.[8]

THE CAMPAIGN

In mid-July the annexation opponents selected two or three tax bills on property recently annexed to the city to "prove" what would happen to property taxes if annexation succeeded. Taxes on these properties increased by 30 per cent after annexation. It was claimed that these were typical tax bills sent to Frantz on the initiative of the taxpayers concerned. These property owners, in spite of paying higher taxes, had no greater police and fire protection than before. The two tax bills were made a part of a large paid political advertisement in the *Suburban News-Shopper,* which is distributed free throughout the annexation area.

About a month later, E. W. Chopson, an employee of the California State Personnel Board and a member of the anti-annexation group, told the Arden-Arcade Rotary Club that annexation would bring a 30 per cent tax increase. Fire protection would be no better, he said, and the area did not need better police protection. Sewers and street lights could be obtained at the same cost, with or without annexation.[9] Frank

Stipak responded to the *Bee*'s account of the speech in a letter
to the editor. The taxation examples being used by anti-annexation spokesmen, he said, were the result of an error on the part
of the county in making out the tax bills in that area. Part of
the county tax was later refunded. Also, in the year before
annexation to Sacramento city the fire district, anticipating
annexation, levied no tax.

In the week following Chopson's appearance, Stanley
Kronick spoke to the Arden-Arcade Rotary Club. He termed
annexation the key to good government; the Sacramento area
was one area, socially, culturally, and economically, and therefore should be one governmentally. He spoke of the downward
trend of the property tax rate in Sacramento and the costs of
the multiplicity of special districts outside of Sacramento. He
stressed that only 50 per cent of Sacramento's expenditures
was paid from the property tax.

At about the same time, J. R. Liske presented a policy statement on annexation to the Carmichael Rotary Club. After
reviewing the process of urbanization and the need for governmental reform, and dismissing the tax issue, Liske presented
some important arguments in support of the annexation. Sacramento, he said, is one of the most sound financially of the
country's municipal organizations and it would be to the advantage of any contiguous area to become a part of it. This annexation would achieve 40 per cent of the task of unifying the entire
urbanized area of Sacramento County and would provide the
impetus for the remaining 60 per cent of the urbanized area to
join Sacramento. This annexation would not interfere with
MGC's recommendation for functional consolidation of services.

Benjamin Frantz wrote a long letter to the city council, on
behalf of the Arden-Arcade Government Committee, which
asked over 30 very specific questions about how annexation
would be carried out—how many policemen will patrol the

area, how many of the present firemen will be retained, and so forth. Sacramento's city manager replied by letter to Frantz's request for an immediate answer. The manager stated that some time would be required to get complete answers to the many detailed questions asked; in the meantime, he sent a copy of the city's official annexation policy, which would answer a number of the queries. The city manager also agreed to speak at a public meeting in the annexation area on September 22.[10] Members of the city council and some other city officials also attended this meeting. Since those strongly opposed to annexation dominated the meeting, this was a harrowing experience for most of the city officials. Many at the meeting seemed more devoted to trying to confound the city representatives than to seeking information.

The *Sacramento Bee* urged the city to move faster in this matter of presenting facts to the voters of the annexation area. In the September 1 issue an editorial stated that the voters were getting plenty of distorted, false, and self-serving misinformation, and this needed to be challenged by the true picture given by governmental officials. The presentation of facts in a precise manner should be a tireless and exhaustive effort, the *Bee* said. Sacramento was indeed supplying specific facts on annexation. During September pro-annexation leaders received reports on how city services are financed, and what annexed areas might expect as to street lighting, sewerage, water supply, storm drainage, and roads and streets.

During the month of September, the *Bee* devoted much space to the annexation issue. Each day at least one lengthy report about the advantages of annexation appeared in a prominent position in the paper. The following headlines typify the type of articles written: "City Offers Parks in North for Less," "Survey Refutes Arden Tax Fears," "Arden-Arcade Park Study Unit Is Urged," "City Promises Street Work If Annexing Wins,"

"City Offers Sewage, Drainage Program," "City Would Raise Fire, Police Protection in Arden-Arcade," "Suburb Will Get Trash Pickup," "Residents of Arden, Arcade Would Have Say in Planning."

About a week before the election the *Sacramento Union* ran a series of three articles on the annexation question, which concluded that there would be little difference in taxes, streets, sidewalks, gutters, sewers, and police and fire protection whether or not annexation succeeded. Only if this annexation were to be followed by other major ones, to unify the entire urban area, would the annexation be beneficial. Annexation opponents were enthusiastic about the *Union* articles, which seemed to confirm that the Arden-Arcade annexation would interfere with, rather than promote, unification of governmental agencies and services.

The several suburban weekly newspapers distributed in the area were openly opposed to annexation. The *Carmichael Westerner*, the *Carmichael Courier*, and the *Suburban News-Shopper*, for example, editorialized against annexation. One of the pro-annexation leaders complained during an interview that these suburban papers "wouldn't even publish the pro-annexation news releases although anti-annexation releases were published regularly."

Some of the Sacramento city councilmen and other city officials who were strongest for annexation stated off the record that the *Bee* presented the advantages of annexation too often and too conspicuously. They reasoned that voters resented being told so persistently what was good for them and began to suspect the motives of the *Bee* and city officials. Large numbers of suburbanites felt that the *Bee*, although liberal on national issues, took a provincial, pro-Sacramento position on local and regional issues. The *Bee's* enthusiasm for annexation led some citizens to adopt the opposite position.

CAMPAIGN FINANCES

The records of the pro-annexation movement showed that contributions totaling slightly under $1,000 were received, and that expenditures were approximately $750. The surplus was transferred to the Sacramento City-County Chamber of Commerce, which had advanced an estimated $500 to $600 additional during the final days of the campaign, mainly for postage, mimeographing expense, and the retention of a public relations firm. The money was collected by a small group of the annexation leaders and came mainly from small individual contributions and from a few businesses in the annexation area and downtown Sacramento. For the most part, businessmen failed to contribute, and this represented a major difficulty in the annexation campaign. While some individual businessmen did give money, they wanted to remain anonymous and did not want to get their companies involved.

No dependable estimate could be obtained of the amount of money the anti-annexation forces collected, the sources from which it came, or the purposes for which it was expended. The treasurer of the anti-annexation forces was unwilling to divulge this information. Only one interviewee (pro-annexation) was willing to make a specific estimate of anti-annexation expenditures. His estimate was $3,000. Others made statements to the effect that one individual was paid $2,000 as a public relations expert and that the postage bill for the anti-annexation group must have exceeded $1,400.

ANTI-ANNEXATION STRATEGY

There were strange bedfellows in the anti-annexation movement. Some of the leaders favored merger of city and county government and concluded that piecemeal annexation would be a retrogressive step. Others were attracted to the movement because it provided the opportunity to forestall the growth of "big government." Some of these were primarily against a big Sacramento; some were, at least originally, against the whole concept of a metropolitan government on ideological grounds. For some, merger was the goal; for others, "home rule" was to be preserved. But whatever the original differences in goals, the leaders adopted a single-minded strategy for opposition.

Throughout the month of September the anti-annexation forces, with the help of a full-time paid public relations man, waged an active campaign. A few annexation opponents made numerous speeches and issued statements for the press almost daily. Newspapers were flooded with letters criticizing the "high and mighty" attitude of Sacramento city officials. Immediately before the election, the area was blanketed with anti-annexation literature which stressed home rule, grass-roots government, and taxes. A two-page "fact sheet" was entitled "If You Can't Afford Higher Taxes Vote No on Annexation." Defeat of annexation, the sheet read, would force city-county consolidation, which in turn would mean economy in government. Although the city's problems were never identified, the sheet stated that they were so numerous and complex that no time could be spent on improvements in Arden-Arcade. The opposition leaders believed that it was sufficient merely to remind the voter of life in the city, with its traffic congestion, slums, delinquency, crime, and racial strife. Apparently they were right.

Annexation opponents also distributed a four-page publication called "Urban Living"—with the subheading, "Dedicated to Progress Unlimited." This pamphlet repeated the charge that annexation means higher taxes. The readers' attention was called to the city's present preoccupation with a proposed freeway, and suggested that until this was resolved the city would have no time for Arden-Arcade's problems. The pamphlet concluded with a request for help in fighting the annexation and accused annexation proponents of making use of a public relations firm, hired to sell Arden-Arcade residents a bill of goods. (In fact, at the time this pamphlet was distributed, no public relations firm had been employed by the annexation organization, and the firm of Queale and Associates, which became involved later, was employed by the City-County Chamber of Commerce, not the annexation committee.) Printed in large block type was the statement, "We Need Annexation Like We Need A Hole in Our Head." Another brochure, mailed to "occupant," stressed the same arguments—home rule, taxation, and the evils of the big city. Anti-annexation posters were tacked on fences and posted on lawns along the major roads of the area during the last four or five days before the election.

PRO-ANNEXATION STRATEGY

In contrast to the great amount of literature distributed by the opponents, annexation advocates prepared only one newspaper tabloid, distributed during the final days before the election. The support of the League of Women Voters and the 8,000 citizens who had signed the petitions, and the endorsement by MGC and the Greater North Area Chamber of Commerce were emphasized. (It was not mentioned that the chamber endorsed the movement over the objections of its Urban Government Committee.) The pamphlet dealt with specific problems in the area such as water supply, sewers and storm drains, and taxation. To reinforce the tax reduction claims, the proponents summarized the results of a survey made recently by a Sacramento bank. The total property taxes paid on 40 homes in Sacramento was $10,355, as compared with $10,464 on 40 comparable homes in Arden-Arcade.

The literature also presented arguments for uniting the governments of two communities that were already one in most other aspects. The persons promoting annexation were introduced as men and women typical of the residents of the area as a whole. They owned modest homes, and were contributing their time plus dimes and dollars to achieve annexation.

The advantages of annexation boiled down to three major ones: Sacramento gets half of its revenue from sources not available to unincorporated areas; the industry and commercial developments within Sacramento would help pay for governmental services in Arden-Arcade; and a large, modern city government can render municipal-type services more efficiently and economically than can the special districts. The pro-annexation document concluded, "Tuesday We Vote; Let's Make Sacramento *Our* City." Unlike their opponents, the annexation leaders did little in the way of lawn signs or posters.

The pro-annexation leaders agreed that no significant differences in philosophy arose among themselves and only minor differences over strategy came up. "On one occasion," one leader stated, "we discussed whether to slug it out or to continue to be calm and objective." Since they were amateurs rather than professional organizers and publicists, however, some weak points in method were inevitable. There were the usual complaints of volunteer workers about their organization —too few did too much of the work with too little financial support. One participant felt that the organization needed the leadership of an experienced businessman and a large number of subordinates taking responsibility for the activities of the movement. Leaders also mentioned the lack of communication between precinct workers and the central organization. There was, in addition, the problem, basic to all reform groups, of effectively and dramatically presenting facts, while anti-reform groups need present only opinions and appeals to the citizens' emotions.

ORGANIZATIONAL SUPPORT FOR ANNEXATION

Annexation advocates made much of the fact that a number of organized groups had voted in support of the movement. The support given by the League of Women Voters and MGC has already been mentioned. The League prepared a leaflet in support of the movement, and League members distributed it. The League's support was based on a desire to reduce the bewildering number of governments, to obtain more services at a reasonable cost, to move toward merger, and to achieve economy in government through functional consolidation. In addition to directing the preparation and distribution of the pro-annexation leaflet, Mrs. Henry Long, president, participated in public forums as the League's spokesman. The Sacramento Area Planning Association also announced its support one week before the election, stating that annexation is "the best immediate approach to the solution of our metropolitan governmental problems."

The Urban Government Committee of the Greater North Area Chamber of Commerce had consistently opposed any extension of the city of Sacramento across the American River, a policy in which the chamber itself had concurred. However, about two weeks before the election, the Sacramento City-County Chamber of Commerce managed to obtain endorsement of annexation by its neighboring chamber. The city-county chamber pointed out that the Arden-Arcade annexation was the first step toward implementation of the recommendations embodied in MGC's final report, namely the annexation to Sacramento of the entire unincorporated, urbanized area of the county. The board of directors of the North Area chamber overrode the negative recommendation of its Urban Government Committee and voted on September 10 to support the annexation proposal. The directors included in their statement of support an endorsement of the MGC plan for mass annexation.[11]

Only the League of Women Voters and the City-County Chamber of Commerce contributed any active help other than public endorsement. The North Area chamber provided no working support and its endorsement was too late to be effective.

The only organizations reported to have given substantial support to anti-annexation workers were the County Sheriff's Association and various fire departments and firemen's associations in the annexation area. It is apparent that those associated with fire protection in the Arden-Arcade annexation area considerably influenced the negative vote, although the full extent of their contribution is not known. Whatever the motives of the individuals, the various fire fighting organizations had the potential time, talent, and other resources, plus personal financial and political incentive, to make them formidable factors in any political decision.

Besides job security and protection of retirement benefits, and the frankly expressed desire of fire chiefs to remain in their positions, reasons given by local fire department members for their opposition were various. They did not want to be controlled by the *Sacramento Bee* and the *Sacramento Union*, which some believed was controlled by the *Bee*. They also expressed fear that big government would lead to socialism or Communism. The fire fighters were convinced that the area was receiving better fire protection now than it would under annexation. The Arden Firemen's Association and several individual firemen and officials are reported to have contributed money to the anti-annexation forces, and many worked actively against annexation. One fireman stated that he and his wife

had spent all of their free time in canvassing the area, telling
the people about the evils of annexation. This fireman, along
with others, had also attended many of the anti-annexation
meetings and had worked closely with Frantz in soliciting signatures. A fire chief claimed to have visited every residence in
the part of his district which was included in the annexation
area. Another fireman reported devoting eight hours a day for
three months to fighting annexation. Those persons in the fire
departments who favored annexation tended to keep their
opinions to themselves.

One interviewee associated a water district and a garbage
collecting agency with the anti-annexation activities. He contended that the same addressograph plates used for water and
garbage collection bills in the area were used to address anti-
annexation literature.

ANNEXATION DEFEATED

The Arden-Arcade annexation was defeated by 11,410 to
6,170 in the September 29 election. The fact that there were
about 1,400 more valid signatures on the annexation petitions
than "yes" votes raises the interesting question—what motives
did people have for signing the petitions? Did some agree to
sign only to bring the issue to a vote or had some voters become
converted to the opposition?

Thirty-nine per cent of the qualified voters did not vote. The
annexation proposal received a majority of votes in only one of
the 60 precincts.

Seemingly, the residents of Arden-Arcade did not feel that
governmental reorganization was necessary. They already were
receiving most of the customary municipal services. The fact
that they had to rely upon several governmental units rather
than upon one for these services, and that possibly they were

paying more for these services than might be the case under annexation did not seem of particular importance to them. The emotional appeal of the opposition, based upon grass roots, local control, and home rule, received a more receptive hearing.

ARDEN-ARCADE ANNEXATION ATTEMPT EVALUATED BY INDIVIDUALS INVOLVED

Previous discussion of the backgrounds of the annexation leaders and their conduct of the annexation campaign indicated that they were, for the most part, concerned with a theoretical notion of better government, which made the abolishment of small, overlapping service districts necessary.

One primary motive of the anti-annexation leaders interviewed was a desire to keep the area "rural." Another interviewee preferred the *status quo* to annexation even if the latter would bring lower taxes. Another of the early leaders argued that annexation to Sacramento would mean a lessening of local representation as well as an increase in taxes. He saw the *Bee* and the "downtown power structure" as obstacles to effective government for Arden-Arcade. During the interview he made several references to a nation-wide "organization" which has repeatedly connected powerful metropolitan government with a Communist conspiracy to destroy democracy. One of the officers of the anti-annexation forces expressed the initial fear of higher taxes, but also expressed distrust of Sacramento merchants. He felt that annexation would result in Arden-Arcade's being taxed excessively so that downtown could be rehabilitated. "After all, redevelopment is a mistake; we've got to have slums. There must be cheap housing in a city. Why not leave it where it is?" Another leader said that even though the *Bee* favored bigness and centralization, and aid to downtown Sacramento, what was good for the city might not necessarily be good for the suburban area.

Leaders on both sides were asked to name community organizations that should have supported their efforts but did not. As might be expected, pro-annexation leaders listed several organizations from which they had expected more active support. Even those groups that had taken a part in the annexation effort, such as the League of Women Voters and the City-County Chamber of Commerce, were criticized for doing too little too late. Leaders felt that merchant groups, educators, PTA's, and improvement clubs ought to have joined in the movement. Lack of support from civic, professional, and service associations was also cited as weakening the cause. The indecision and division in the North Area chamber was most often mentioned as a decisive factor in the defeat of annexation.

> The North Area chamber should have been a spark plug to the annexation movement, but it failed to accept the Metropolitan Government Committee's report. This existing organization should have assumed leadership and there should not have been a superimposed annexation committee. It was the opposition of the North Area chamber that really defeated our movement. This organization is comprised mainly of small businessmen, but the attorneys therein apparently are the most interested in governmental reform and their recommendations have usually been followed. Most of these attorneys were opposed to annexation. Why the attorneys behaved this way, I am not sure, but I suppose they deem that it is not wise to be associated with a losing cause, and in thinking this way they, indeed, make governmental reform a losing cause. The small businessmen in and out of the chamber were the most timid of all I came across. We got very little money from small businessmen. Our $50 checks came from bigger businesses. The little businessman would not rock the boat. Maybe it was because he was just getting started in business. Also, much of the Northeast area business is handled by big chains, and the managers of the branches had no special community ties. Many of the businessmen feared change and this is a function of ignorance.

The answers reveal personal disappointment in the failure of organizations to rally in support of annexation, and the leaders' perceptiveness of attitudes and values in both the suburbs and the city. This understanding of the community, however, seems to have been gained through their experience in the annexation movement.

Surprisingly, the victors were not fully satisfied with the organized support they received. They too listed the PTA's, chambers of commerce, local improvement and service clubs, and professional associations as groups that should have lent support to their cause.

Pro-annexation leaders were agreed that there were influential citizens in the Sacramento area whose participation in the annexation movement might have been expected at the beginning and whose support would have improved the chances for the movement's success. But, for the most part, there is little consistency among the leaders in their selection of names of individuals or groups of persons that were generally regarded as influential. Downtown businessmen, the managers of two large shopping centers in the northeast area, bank officials, and industrial executives all were mentioned as potential sources of support that did not materialize. Influential citizens in these occupations were approached by annexation leaders but they expressed indifference and sometimes opposition to governmental reform. The conservatism of the business and industrial leaders was attributed to their desire to avoid any controversy that might alienate customers and to the stable employment situation in Sacramento, which gives these people a relatively secure income. Some businessmen who favored annexation did not participate in the movement because, in one person's words, "they did not realize the importance of annexation to their own self-interest." They were also overconfident that the movement would succeed. One annexation leader doubted that there were any "influential people" in Sacramento, an expression which gives further evidence to the fact that Sacramento lacks any widely recognized leadership.

The responses by anti-annexation leaders to the question concerning failure of influential people to participate in the countermovement were rather bland. One interviewee proclaimed, "Why, every influential person should have been involved," but, after a short pause, asked, "But who in the area are influential?" These people, whoever they may be, failed to support anti-annexation because of "business" reasons and general apathy. "Businessmen did not want to become embroiled. They felt their businesses would be better off if they stayed out." One leader estimated that no more than "10 to 12 per cent" of the area's inhabitants became involved in the annexation attempt. "The people are not interested. The issue must be close to them. They take government for granted. They gripe about taxes and weather but do nothing about either."

The leaders were asked about the reactions of specific groups and organizations in the area. All identified the *Bee* as favorable to annexation. Two annexation leaders credited the *Bee* with altruistic motives for its stand, but most said simply that the *Bee* had always maintained an annexation policy. The anti-annexation leaders explained the *Bee*'s stand by its traditional alignment with "downtown and the incumbent city government." Some also felt the *Bee* "didn't want another major newspaper" in the area. In spite of its position, one interviewee said that the *Bee* "actually did more to *get* votes for us than *lose* them." This leader did acknowledge the *Bee*'s "generally honest coverage," including news items "detrimental to its editorial policy." The rejection of annexation by the weeklies in the northeast area was generally interpreted as allegiance to suburban advertising. One reported that there was a desire to convert the weeklies into big city dailies. Another predicted that probably the *Suburban News-Shopper* would emerge as a daily paper to compete with the *Bee*. It was assumed that this could happen only if the North Area had its own identity as a separate big community rather than being a part of Sacramento city.

School personnel were regarded as "neutral" and "mixed" or "namby-pamby." One annexation leader reported that "teachers were afraid to sign petitions because of possible reaction of school administrators," but another felt that the officials were neutral while the teachers were opposed to annexation.

Most annexation leaders believed that among real estate people the decision about annexation was "primarily an individual matter." Probably the most perceptive comment was that "real estate brokers were favorable, developers unfavorable" for the reason that "although city and county building codes are similar, the city enforces its codes more effectively, and therefore it is understandable that the developers might not want annexation."

Only one annexation leader felt that the businessmen from Sacramento were unfavorably inclined, and that was because they "feared higher taxes in underwriting of the bedroom area." Another insisted that the businessmen did not make their position known. But all other annexation leaders interviewed felt that the downtown businessmen were pro-annexation; annexation would increase downtown prosperity. While acknowledging support, one leader complained that the businessmen's leadership "didn't show at all." The anti-annexation leaders interpreted the position of city businesses as a way of coping with suburban competition. Annexation would make it possible for the merchants to "flood the area with buses and to try to get the customers to go downtown." Another anti-annexation leader stated that downtown interests wanted to control

outlying business through city government. Suburban businessmen failed to support either group in order to avoid taking a
controversial stand, leaders on both sides of the issue said.

The pro-annexation leaders interviewed generally agreed
that Sacramento city officials favored annexation. Reasons
given for this support were both altruistic and protective. The
officials felt a "sense of responsibility to the entire community";
they believed "the city, not the county or a new city in the
northeast area, should be the base for the vast metropolitan
area" and an annexation policy should be pursued even though
it would cost the city money. From another point of view, "a
bigger city has greater prestige." One interviewee stated, however, that in informal conversation city department heads had
expressed "fear of tax increase within the existing city," and he
also "guessed" that the city transit authority, aware of the costs
of extending bus service to Arden-Arcade, had many doubts
about the venture. These unofficial reservations about annexation were perceived by the opposition also: "Many city officials,
especially those beneath the top ranks, didn't care, and many
probably did not want an annexation." Most opposition leaders,
however, felt that annexation had firm support from city officials, who, they said, hoped for "bigger empires."

County officials were unfavorably inclined toward the annexation movement. Annexation would mean a "waning prestige of
county officials" and some county workers were severely repri-
manded for becoming involved in the movement in any way. It
was reported, though, that "the top appointive officials" thought
annexation was a good step, but, as one anti-annexation leader
put it, "they didn't dare express themselves openly." Nor were
they willing to publicize their opposition to annexation.

The League of Women Voters supported annexation after a
formal study of local government. Its previous promotion of the
pas report and city-county merger was not looked upon as

inconsistent with support for annexation, and leading proponents interpreted its position as considered and sincere. Annexation opponents felt the League had taken a partisan position,
however: League members are "radicals," "a bunch of Democrats." "The League was misguided although sincere. It turned
partisan on this issue, although its constitution says it should
not." One opponent admitted that "the League was unfavorable
to us for academic and theoretical reasons." In spite of these
references to "partisanship," it should be noted again that the
annexation issue was not one of Democrats versus Republicans. By coincidence, some of the annexation leaders also were
active in the Democratic Party while some of the annexation
opponents were active in the Republican Party.

All of the annexation and the anti-annexation leaders interviewed were asked why the Arden-Arcade annexation proposal
had been rejected by the voters. The annexation leaders,
usually after a moment of embarrassed silence, gave the following range of explanations: "the shoe isn't pinching";
"there's a natural resistance to change"; "the citizens remained
poorly informed." Annexation leaders also recognized that they
had failed to counter the opposition on the tax issue in an
effective way. "The anti-annexation forces knowingly confused
issues with half-truths and mis-truths." Their group was hampered by too little time and money and poor organization. The
suburban antagonism to the *Bee* was mentioned again as a
factor leading to defeat.

Members of the defeated annexation group recognized that
one basic cause of their failure was that the residents in the
area were pretty well satisfied with their situation at the
moment. "The people were just not unhappy enough," one person said. The annexation opponents readily admitted that this
complacency was one decisive factor in their favor. This prevailing attitude, combined with an antagonism toward the city

and a desire for self-identity, made up the ingredients for defeat of annexation. In addition, the opponents admitted to confusing the issues on purpose. Their slogan was, "If In Doubt, Vote NO." "Obviously," as one said, "we were quite successful."

CONCLUSIONS

There was a reasonably satisfactory level of municipal-type services in Arden-Arcade, although it was governed by a conglomeration of special districts. Those who anticipated an ultimate breakdown of services because of this system were unable to communicate their concern to the satisfied residents. In addition, the property taxation issue proved vital. The opposition pressed its tax claims—which were based on a few, carefully selected cases—much more vigorously than did the proponents. Although annexation leaders showed through their study that the effect of annexation would be more and better services for the same price, taxpayers tend to be fearful of tax increases and are more willing to believe those who forecast higher taxes. The effects of annexation upon governmental organization were also poorly explained. Annexation, as described by its opponents, meant adding another layer of government—and another tax collector—on top of the many already in existence. The proponents failed to emphasize that as special districts are eliminated the governmental structure would be simplified.

Citizens were suspicious of the annexation leaders' claims. They were told that they would get added services without increase in taxes, but surely this could not be. Annexation proponents failed to get across the fact that their area would have new sources of income after annexation—from the local sales tax, gasoline tax, liquor licenses, motor vehicle license fees, and so on.

Residents of this suburban area were very jealous of their local autonomy; a lot of small governments meant that they had grass-roots government. This, of course, is a basic principle of the American system, which some of the annexation opponents exploited by warning that a new form of government called "metro" was being advocated by Communist-tinged organizations. It did not matter that many of the voters apparently were unaware of the existence of all of the units of government to which they were subject, that they did not bother to vote for officials of these numerous governments, and that they did not know where the business of these governments was being transacted. It still was grass-roots government. One of the proponents, in diagnosing the defeat, suggested that, because FHA and other mortgages now provide for a monthly lump sum payment of both mortgage and local taxes, most citizens do not know how much the many districts collect in taxes.

Sacramento's image had been damaged by the many years when the city followed rigidly the letter of the law on annexation, which said that proposals must originate in the areas to be annexed. With the exception of the Oak Park annexation in 1911, there were no annexations to Sacramento until the middle 1940's. By the time Sacramento began to show active interest in annexation the population clusters beyond its borders had developed feelings of local identity. Sacramento, the city, can be distinguished from Sacramento, the community. When suburbanites travel, they undoubtedly speak of themselves as Sacramentans, but at home they look with suspicion upon the city of Sacramento. A number of persons conceded that annexation was more logical than whatever other arrangements they were advocating at the moment, but "Sacramento doesn't want us," "Sacramento isn't interested in us," or "Sacramento wants to grab only the highly assessed property." They also did not want to become involved in the city's problems such as the deteriorated west end and the rising percentages of minority groups in the city. Some pictured Sacramento as a "cold" city, which accepted police brutality as typical of the city policemen, and saw the city manager as an efficient but cold administrator.

The efforts of firemen in the northeast area were important. The firemen, operating from an already existing organization and fearful of the effect of annexation upon their jobs, provided the mechanism for getting house-to-house coverage with anti-annexation materials. They prepared and put up the "Don't Annex" posters and signs. They also contributed money to the cause. Although the proponents of annexation set up an elaborate organization on paper, their leadership base was narrow and only a very small number of persons really worked at it. Thus, success of the firemen's loosely knit organization reinforces the conclusion that few effective organizations exist in the northeast area.

The position taken by the Urban Government Committee of the Greater North Area Chamber of Commerce was influential. Neither the committee nor the chamber now exists, but the committee had an important effect on the thinking of the people northeast of the American River during its existence. The committee was wedded to the idea of city-county merger. It proposed something of the sort before PAS did and after that sat in judgment upon every proposal for governmental change in metropolitan Sacramento. It was sure to oppose any proposal that would enhance the position of the city of Sacramento. While the Greater North Area Chamber of Commerce finally endorsed the proposed Arden-Arcade annexation, its Urban Government Committee never did.

The leadership role of Dr. James R. Cowan was believed by some to have been crucial. Many of those who worked for annexation felt that if Cowan had supported this annexation wholeheartedly it would have received wider approval in the northeast area. Cowan, who had been a leader in the Urban Government Committee, SMAAC, and MGC, had supported first city-county merger and later large-scale annexation to Sacramento. As a prominent figure in the northeast area, Cowan could perhaps have swayed some citizens if he had expressed his approval more vigorously. It is difficult to judge the influence, manifest and potential, of one individual. While it is doubtful that active support from Cowan could have reversed the outcome of the election, the fact that some pro-annexation people believed that Cowan could have expressed such influence is another commentary on the lack of area-wide leadership.

The skill of modern public relations and propaganda utilized by annexation opponents was not matched by the proponents of annexation. Defenders of the *status quo* had the advantage —and retained it.

Perhaps more fundamental than these local issues is the changing character of American metropolises in general and the Sacramento metropolitan area in particular. Sacramento is a vivid example of extra-community influences which have become increasingly important in metropolises throughout the country. Many of the business leaders are hardly more than bureaucratic transients. Local bankers, long identified as stalwarts of the communities, are no longer local, but are career professionals in state-wide organizations. They may find themselves in strange, or at least new, communities from year to year. (California's larger bank organizations operate branch banks in many of the communities throughout the state.) More and more of the leading merchants are executives of chain stores, who are also likely to be transferred often. Con-

servatism, timidity, and calculated neutralism are thus built
into the leadership in the business community. The reluctance
of businessmen to take a stand on annexation was reported
repeatedly by movement leaders, pro and con. This "neutrality," combined with Sacramento's dependence on state government rather than local enterprises, and on federal military and
contract installations rather than local industries for the back-
bone of its economy, makes more apparent the reasons why
neither effective leadership nor enthusiastic interest in governmental reform has been displayed.

The following letter, written to the *Sacramento Bee* about a
week after the proposal was defeated, is perhaps the best summary of the situation:

> Now that the victorious opponents have gloated piously
> of a mandate for merger and the defeated proponents
> have swallowed their pride in brave rationalizations, let
> us consider the real reasons why annexation failed in the
> Arden-Arcade area. First is fear based on ignorance. Un-
> able to resolve the tax question, people feared the worst
> and voted no. Second is suspicion. The motives of those
> who promote change are always suspect. People elect to
> live with the evils they have rather than take a chance on
> those they know not of. Third is self-interest. Jobs and
> prestige based on the status quo outweigh the public
> welfare. Finally there is the skill of "public relations" in
> exploiting these weaknesses—fear, ignorance, suspicion,
> and cupidity. So annexation was not defeated on its mer-
> its, and there was no mandate for merger or for anything
> else.[12]

In the Hagginwood-Del Paso Heights annexation area the
potential advantages of annexation to the inhabitants were
easily seen. In the Arden-Arcade annexation area the potential advantages did not stand out so clearly. This perhaps ex-

plains why the Hagginwood-Del Paso Heights proposal was defeated by a very narrow vote whereas the Arden-Arcade proposal was overwhelmingly put down. Practically all of the Hagginwood-Del Paso Heights annexation area is a part of Sacramento city today, while most of the Arden-Arcade area still is outside Sacramento's boundaries.

6

Sacramento Leaders and Metropolitan Affairs

This chapter describes and analyzes some of the characteristics, attitudes, and views of those persons who were considered to have been influential in the community but who did not participate directly in any of the governmental reorganization attempts. The same kind of information is then given about the leaders of the various study and reorganization attempts, and the movements are compared. In the third part, some important questions related to leadership in metropolitan Sacramento are considered.

GENERAL COMMUNITY LEADERS

Following Floyd Hunter's general approach, the authors located leaders by means of reputation—that is, the attribution of influence.[1] During personal interviews, 18 "judges" were asked two questions:

> Whom would you consider the ten most powerful and influential people in the whole Sacramento metropolitan area—that is, the real leaders?
>
> Thinking back over the 1950's, whom would you consider the most influential people in relation to the problem of changes in governmental organization in the Sacramento metropolitan area? Name five from the city of Sacramento. Name five from the remainder of the Sacramento metropolitan area.

The 18 judges, chosen by the authors, included a city official, a county official, a newspaperman, a legislator, a newspaper editor, two school superintendents, a judge, two officers of women's organizations, a Negro leader, a religious leader, a labor union official, a banker, a real estate man, two chamber of commerce officials, and a state official. They were assured that their nominations would be treated as confidential information.

The judges were individuals who the authors believed would be in the best position to provide an informed opinion about leadership in the area. One of the persons invited to be a judge declined. Another, who accepted, named only persons in official elective or appointive positions despite our instructions to avoid this. Since this approach to nomination of leaders did not agree with the intent of the question, the nominations by this judge in response to the first question were not considered. Several other judges expressed reservations about their ability to answer the first question about the "real leaders" although all eventually submitted names. A few commented that this would have been an easier question to answer 25 years ago. From the judges' responses the individuals to be interviewed as "general community leaders" and some of the leaders of particular movements were selected.

We did not find a clearly identified central power group of any sort—no small elite of businessmen such as Hunter identified in Regional City. While the results are not strictly comparable—different questions were asked and slightly different methods of obtaining nominations were employed—it seems clear that Hunter found much greater agreement among his judges than we did among ours.

In response to the first question about the "real leaders" only four of the judges named exactly ten individuals. Nine named more than ten; five named fewer than ten. The range was from zero to 37, with a median of 10.5. In all, 227 nominations were made by the 18 judges. The most frequent mention of one individual in response to the first question was eight times. One individual received seven nominations; two received six; five received five; eight received four; 98 received three or fewer nominations.

Of the 28 persons who were nominated by three or more of our judges, 14 were businessmen (including four bankers); three, department store executives; two, insurance executives; one, a newspaper publisher; one, an insurance agent; one, a realtor; one, a supermarket executive; and one, a defense industry executive. Eight nominees were government officials: two city officials, three county officials, one state official, one state assemblyman, and one congressman. The remaining six persons included two religious leaders, two attorneys, one school administrator, and one newspaper editor. Since state government is a major employer in the Sacramento area, it is significant that only two state officials were nominated, neither of whom was active in any of the governmental reorganization movements studied.

Of the 24 who received two or more nominations in response

to the question about governmental reorganization leaders, 13 were also nominated at least twice as general community leaders. Thus there is some overlap between the two groups, but the majority of those who are considered influential in the community have not been active in reorganization attempts, and conversely. The overlap between the responses to the two questions might have been caused by two aspects of the interviewing technique. The questions were asked during the course of a single interview, and the same names may have occurred to the respondent in answering both questions. Secondly, since the interviews were conducted after the reorganization attempts, some nominees, not acknowledged as leaders in the past, may have attained general community prominence as a result of their governmental reorganization activities.

All persons interviewed were asked to list names of individuals whose support would be especially important in securing voter approval of a county-wide referendum—"for example, a proposal to reorganize the governments of the Sacramento metropolitan area." Of the 21 individuals who were nominated by two or more interviewees, 13 were among the top 28 nominated independently by the 18 judges as general community leaders and seven were among the top 24 nominated by the judges as influential with respect to governmental reorganization. Here again we see partial agreement in identifying influential Sacramentans. Since the overlap is substantially greater for the "ten most powerful and influential leaders" than for reorganization leaders, this gives added support to the contention that the reorganization efforts were not able to attract the community's top leadership.

In using the "nomination" approach a great deal hinges upon the judges chosen. Their nominations reflect their own special points of view, and a different set of judges might very well result in a different set of leaders. The more homogeneous the judges the more likely their lists of leaders will agree. A rough measure of the degree of agreement among our judges was obtained by dividing the judges at random into two groups and by noting the degree of overlap obtained in identifying the top 15 Sacramento leaders. When this was done the two groups agreed on only six of the 15 leaders, a fact which indicates a low degree of agreement among the judges.

Of the 28 individuals receiving the greatest number of nominations as community-wide leaders, nine were known to have been active in connection with one or another of the reorganization movements. Since most of these nine persons active in the reorganization movements were to be interviewed in any case, we selected 14 of the remaining group to be interviewed as individuals influential in the community at large but not active in any of the movements studied.[2]

These 14 general community leaders included four bankers, two religious leaders, three department store executives, an insurance agent, a supermarket executive, an insurance company executive, a realtor, and a lawyer.

VIEWS OF METROPOLITAN PROBLEMS

All interviewees were asked, "What seem to you to be the most important problems in the Sacramento metropolitan area?" Responses of all 96 interviewees are summarized in Table 2. The five most important problems as seen by the 14 general community leaders were: traffic and parking (seven mentions), long-range area-wide planning (four mentions), and industrial development, schools, and sewage disposal and drainage (three mentions each). The general community leaders gave greater emphasis to sewage disposal and drainage, schools, core area development, industrial development, and traffic and parking, and less emphasis to multiplicity of special districts and to governmental reorganization than did the total group of interviewees. The most marked difference was traffic

TABLE 2

Sacramento Area Problems Viewed as Most
Important by 96 Leaders

Problem	Per Cent Mentioning
Multiplicity of special districts	26
Long-range area wide planning	26
Governmental reorganization	22
Consolidation of governmental services	17
Tax rates	14
Traffic and parking	13
Streets and roads	12
Problems generated by rapid growth	12
Tax base	12
Community spirit	10
Sewage disposal and drainage	10
Industrial development	8
Functions of city and county unclear	8
Continuing community leadership	8
Schools	6
Mass transportation	6
Water	6
Law enforcement	5
Parks and recreation	5
Freeways and arterials	3
Redevelopment	3

and parking, which 50 per cent of the general community leaders spontaneously mentioned as a problem, in contrast to only 12 per cent of the total group. The higher proportion of downtown business leaders among the general community leaders group probably explains this concern. The less frequent mention of problems connected with multiplicity of special districts and with governmental reorganization is consistent with that group's relatively inactive role in reorganization movements.

After the respondent indicated the problems that seemed most important to him, he was asked to select from a list of 23 problems each of the ones he considered an area-wide problem, and to assign the degree of importance of each problem selected. The general community leaders' scores were very similar to those for the group as a whole. There was only one item—zoning—for which the scores differed more than .5 of a point. This agreement was true even for the several items (sewage disposal and drainage, schools, multiplicity of special districts, and industrial development) on which they differed in the first question. This may have occurred because an open-ended question taps a somewhat different dimension than a question asking for degree of importance of each item on a list. The first elicits the salience of problems, the readiness with which they occur to the respondent; the second allows the person to assign a high rating to an item he had not thought of in replying to the open-ended question. Another complicating factor is the high scores—between 3.3 and 3.5—of most of the problems. The scoring method was as follows: "very important" equals 4, "moderately important" equals 3, "of little importance" equals 2, and "don't know" equals 1. Perhaps providing a larger number of alternative ratings would have produced more marked differences among problems.

The general community leaders were somewhat more satisfied with the county government than were the interviewees as a whole—71 per cent as compared with 60 per cent. More were dissatisfied with the county than with the city of Sacramento. Among the county's strong points eight specifically mentioned the county executive. "Excellent administrator," "realistic," "competent," "well trained," were typical comments. A number commented that the county government had been honest, free from graft and corruption. Among the weak points, six indicated that the "pay-as-you-go" approach failed to cope with the population boom in the area, and they were pleased that the county road-building bond issue had passed. A few commented unfavorably about supervisors who were poorly qualified or politically ambitious. Others felt that the caliber of supervisors had improved in recent years.

All of the general community leaders were satisfied with the government of the city of Sacramento, in contrast to 69 per cent of the interviewees as a whole. Eight of the 14 were particularly pleased with the city administration, and mentioned the department heads as well as the city manager. Five commented that the city provides good services, four that the city government is honest, three that the city has had good councilmen, and three that the city is financially sound, with reasonable taxes and low bonded indebtedness.

COMMUNITY LEADERS AND REORGANIZATION

Ten of the 14 general community leaders indicated that they had not been asked to take an active role in any of the reorganization movements. One commented that he lived in the city and so was not directly involved. Another businessman said he avoided becoming involved because of the bitter feelings and "we want to do business with all groups." He had considered running for the school board in another city but when his superior at the bank suggested that he might regret it later on, he decided not to run. He felt this was a wise decision since a school dispute later divided the community into opposing camps. One of the religious leaders, who had been asked to endorse some of the annexation proposals, had declined, feeling that this was not appropriate for him.

Many of the general community leaders felt that the movements helped citizens become aware of the metropolitan problems and showed that people were concerned. "We can't sit quietly and let the city become decadent. The movements are signs that something is going on; they are steps along the way." One respondent suggested that the movements had been great for the press, especially the *Sacramento Bee*. He described them as battles of the press. The public is not greatly concerned about the problem, but the *Bee* is, and he felt that many people were active in the movements in order to obtain the *Bee's* support for their political ambitions.

Most of the general community leaders reported that they did not give any money or services to the reorganization movements or their opposition. Only two reported contributions to annexation proposals; another two reported contributions to the recent campaign for a county bond issue.

Nearly all of the general community leaders had discussed the reorganization movements with city and county officials, business associates, and friends but, for the most part, only in occasional, informal conversations. Only four of the respondents reported discussing the movements with newspaper publishers or editors.

When asked, "What has kept the governmental reorganization idea alive in spite of the failure of several major movements?" seven of the community leaders pointed out that the problems that the movements were designed to overcome continued to exist. The activity of concerned individuals who continue to call the community's attention to its unfinished business was mentioned by several leaders. Four respondents called attention to the actions of the news media, especially the *Sacramento Bee,* and three mentioned the chamber of commerce.

Some leaders, when asked about more effective methods of getting action on metropolitan problems, suggested greater use of existing organizations such as the chambers of commerce, the League of Women Voters, and various service clubs. Others stressed the need for a better cross section of supporters, a broader community base. A few felt that the reorganization movements had not drawn the top leadership in the community, and they contrasted them with the board of directors of the Sacramento Redevelopment Agency (in charge of downtown urban renewal activities), which was composed of citizens who, in their judgment, were widely known and respected.

Some stressed the need for more extensive public information programs through television, newspapers, and public forums, to clarify issues through more complete and less biased analysis. Successful governmental reorganization must be a long-range effort, perhaps requiring a well financed and well directed staff. Some felt that the schools could do a more effective job in imparting a sense of active civic responsibility instead of "viewing from the sidelines." Too often, one respondent said, those who plan programs are not those who must implement them, and more of the public officials should be involved in early planning discussions. Another respondent blamed the large number of absentee owners in Sacramento. The local managers cannot make decisions without checking with the home office, and are not very concerned about Sacramento's long-range interests anyway because they expect to be transferred to another city in a few years.

One respondent was very pessimisitic about achieving marked changes:

> When I was first elected to the city council, I had the naive idea that if a proposal was good it would be accepted. We hired lots of experts—engineers, traffic men, who would study a problem for months and make recommendations. However, someone would always oppose. They would show how the expert plan was all wrong, usually because it ran across the critic's property. I don't see how the press could do more than they are doing already. I'm afraid we can't do much more than we are now doing. I think we are progressing pretty well.

COMPARISONS AMONG SACRAMENTO LEADERS

Chapters Two through Five are based primarily upon personal interviews with movement leaders and upon newspaper accounts of the movements. The first section of this chapter reviews the results of the interviews with general community leaders. The present section compares the information obtained from the Leadership Questionnaire and the Allport-Vernon-Lindzey "Study of Values," which were left with the interviewee to be filled out at his convenience and mailed to the study director.

For purposes of this analysis the interviewees were assigned to one of the following nine groups:

SMAAC and MGC leaders
Pro-incorporation leaders
Anti-incorporation leaders
Pro-annexation leaders in Hagginwood-Del Paso Heights
Anti-annexation leaders in Hagginwood-Del Paso Heights
Pro-annexation leaders in Arden-Arcade
Anti-annexation leaders in Arden-Arcade
General community leaders
X group leaders

In addition to persons who were closely identified with particular movements and general community leaders, the authors interviewed a miscellaneous group of officials and reporters who were knowledgeable about several movements though not direct participants in any. This group has been called the X group. Five members of the X group were city or county officials, five were active in chamber of commerce efforts in the metropolitan government area, and two were newspapermen.

The reader should bear in mind that one-fourth of the interviewees did not complete the questionnaires. The losses were heaviest among the smaac-mgc and the X group leaders, and the results for these groups should be regarded with special caution. The returns from the other movements are reasonably complete. Since only two anti-incorporation leaders were interviewed, that movement has been omitted in the cross-movement comparisons included in this section, but data from these two individuals have been incorporated into the study of the characteristics of the leaders as a whole. The Hagginwood-Del Paso Heights group had a moderately high proportion of returns, but the small number of individuals who returned the questionnaires (4 for the pro-group and 5 for the anti-group) should be remembered when studying the results for these groups. (See Table 3.)

The interview and questionnaire material was obtained after rather than during the active period of the movements. Distortions of memory and hindsight presented as foresight are possible errors. On the other hand, the interviewees may have been more candid about certain past events than they would have been at the time of the event.

BIOGRAPHICAL CHARACTERISTICS OF LEADERS

Most of the leaders are between 40 and 60 years of age. The Arden-Arcade, new city incorporation, and X group members are younger than average. In the case of the first two, this difference probably reflects the relative youth of the residents generally in the areas. The leaders come primarily from the professional and managerial occupations, and more than half of the respondents have had professional or graduate training. smaac-mgc, the new city incorporation group, and the anti-annexation group in Arden-Arcade have very high proportions of leaders with professional or graduate training.

Almost all of the leaders are married and 58 per cent have one or more children under 18 years of age. A higher propor-

tion of the pro-incorporation group and the anti-annexation
leaders in Arden-Arcade have young children. About two-
thirds of the leaders are Protestant. The general community

TABLE 3

Number of Leaders Interviewed and Number Returning
Questionnaire Materials For Each Movement

Movement	Number Interviewed	Number of Questionnaires Returned	Per cent of Questionnaires Returned
SMAAC-MGC	16	9	56
Pro-incorporation	18	16	89
Anti-incorporation	2	2	100
Pro-annexation, Hagginwood-Del Paso Heights	6	4	67
Anti-annexation, Hagginwood-Del Paso Heights	7	5	71
Pro-annexation, Arden-Arcade	11	9	82
Anti-annexation, Arden-Arcade	9	9	100
General community leaders	14	12	86
X group	12	7	58
Total	95*	71	
Per cent of total			75

*Altogether 96 persons were interviewed. One of those interviewed
concerning the Hagginwood-Del Paso Heights annexation movement was
neither for nor against.

leaders have a higher proportion of Catholics than the group
of leaders as a whole. With the exception of the general community leaders, the majority of the interviewees were not born
in the city of Sacramento or even in California. Most of them,
however, have resided in the Sacramento area for nine or more
years. More of the pro-incorporation group and pro-annexation

leaders in Arden-Arcade are relatively new to the Sacramento area.

For the most part, the annexation leaders were living in the area to be annexed at the time of the interviews. Most of the general community leaders lived in the city of Sacramento. Ninety per cent of the leaders doubted whether they would move out of the area in the next three to five years.

As one might assume, many of those who became active in governmental reorganization movements have an extensive background of participation in governmental affairs. Forty-four per cent of the leaders have held elective or appointive office. Public officeholding is less common among pro-annexation leaders in Arden-Arcade and pro-incorporation leaders and relatively more common among general community leaders, three of whom have held three or more such offices.

INTERESTS AND VALUES OF THE LEADERS

In addition to the Leadership Questionnaire, interviewees were asked to complete the Allport-Vernon-Lindzey "Study of Values," a 45-item inventory which is designed to measure the relative prominence of six basic interests or motives: the theoretical, economic, aesthetic, social, political, and religious. The classification is based directly upon Eduard Spranger's *Types of Men*. According to Spranger, a person can be better understood through knowledge of his interests and intentions rather than of his achievements.[3]

In comparison with the general norms provided by Allport, Vernon, and Lindzey, based on scores of 8,369 college students, our leaders have above average theoretical, political, and economic interests and below average social service, aesthetic, and religious interests. Since equal weight was given to the norms for the two sexes, and only seven of our interviewees were female, the norm for the college men group may be a more appropriate basis for comparison. Here the differences are much smaller. Our leaders have significantly lower social service scores and significantly higher theoretical scores. None of the other differences is statistically significant.

With these two exceptions, the mean AVL scores earned by our leaders as a whole are similar to those earned by the 5,894 college men in the AVL norm group. The differences in political, economic, aesthetic, and religious interests from the general norms appear to reflect primarily typical sex differences in interests. The higher theoretical interest found is consistent with the group's concern about long-range area-wide planning, consolidation of governmental services, and the problem of multiplicity of special districts. None of the 21 community problems most frequently volunteered by the leaders is of a social service nature. These leaders are not out to improve conditions at the county hospital, for instance, even though grand juries have found unsatisfactory conditions there.

Are there significant differences among the interests of the various movements? Analysis of variance of AVL scores, arranged by movement, reveals no statistically significant differences among movements. Though there are differences in mean scores between movements, there is also considerable variability within movements.

READING HABITS OF LEADERS

Most leaders reported reading some mass circulation news magazine (*Time, Newsweek,* or *U.S. News*). This was least true of the pro-annexation groups, however. A much smaller proportion of the leaders reported reading a liberal news magazine such as *The Reporter, The Nation,* or *The New Republic.* The groups that were less likely to read a mass circulation magazine were more likely to read a liberal news magazine, but the proportion reading a liberal magazine did not exceed

50 per cent in any of the movements. *Business Week, Wall Street Journal, Fortune,* and other business publications were read most frequently by the pro-annexation group in Arden-Arcade and the general community leaders, and least frequently by both Hagginwood groups. More people from the anti-annexation group in Arden-Arcade and the general community leader groups read intellectual magazines such as *Harpers* or *The Saturday Review,* and fewer from the anti-annexation group in Hagginwood and the X group. Individuals in all groups reported reading some out-of-city newspapers, but the largest proportions were among the general community leaders and the pro-incorporation group. Few in either Hagginwood group read out-of-town papers.

The leaders as a group seem well informed. Fifty-eight per cent read four or more periodicals regularly. Extensive reading is particularly characteristic of the general community leaders.

INTEREST IN COMMUNITY ACTIVITIES

To find out their interest in various community activities, we asked leaders to grade a list of various activities. Half of these were given mean ratings of "moderately interested" or higher, including political, redevelopment, industrial development, international relations, sports and recreational, banking and finance, and study and cultural. The respondents indicated little interest in fraternal activities and veterans' affairs.

The differences among the movements suggest that groups favoring reorganization of some kind have leaders who are more generally active and interested in a variety of community activities. The contrast between the two Hagginwood groups is pronounced. The general community leaders, who come primarily from the city of Sacramento, reiterate their strong interest in redevelopment while anti-annexation leaders in

Hagginwood and Arden-Arcade continue to show indifference to the problem.

VIEWS OF PROBLEMS IN SACRAMENTO

In the opening question in the personal interview, in which each leader was free to identify and describe whatever problems seemed most important to him, most of the leaders mentioned only a few problems. The interviewer took notes on these responses and the results were summarized and assigned, to the extent possible, to a list of categories previously prepared by the investigators. Table 2 indicates the percentage of interviewees selecting each of the 21 most frequently mentioned problems.

The relative lack of agreement on problems is evident in the interview results. The most frequently mentioned problem, multiplicity of special districts, is noted by only 28 per cent of the interviewees. In part, of course, this may be related to the small number of problems mentioned by the typical interviewee. Also, many of the problems have to do with governmental organization rather than with governmental function. For example, the problem perceived is that the Sacramento area has "too many special districts," not that certain functions are not performed at all or are performed inadequately or inefficiently by special districts. This tendency was most characteristic of the pro-annexation leaders in Arden-Arcade and least characteristic of the general community leaders.

After receiving the interviewee's free response answer to the question about problems facing Sacramento, the interviewer handed the respondent a previously prepared list of 23 problems. He was asked to rate each as Very Important, Moderately Important, Of Little or No Importance, or Don't Know. (See Table 4.) When the interviewees' responses to the prepared list of problems are analyzed, agreement among interviewees seems more apparent than suggested by the results in Table 2. The average rating on the first 18 problems in Table 4 is "moderately important" or higher.

TABLE 4

Leaders' Ratings of Degree of Importance
of Area-wide Problems

Problem	Mean Rating*
Long-range area-wide planning	3.8
Consolidation of governmental services	3.6
Freeways and arterials	3.6
Multiplicity of special districts	3.5
Sewage disposal and drainage	3.5
Streets and roads	3.5
Tax base	3.5
Zoning	3.5
Continuing community leadership	3.4
Industrial development	3.4
Tax rates	3.4
Mass transportation	3.3
Parks and recreation	3.3
Schools	3.3
Community spirit	3.1
Refuse disposal	3.1
Law enforcement	3.0
Public health	3.0
Core area development	2.9
Redevelopment	2.9
Cultural activity	2.8
Fire protection	2.8
Racial minority problems	2.5

* This is the mean score assigned the problem by 96 interviewees where "very important" equals 4, "moderately important" equals 3, "of little or no importance" equals 2, and "don't know" equals 1.

Long-range area-wide planning, consolidation of governmental services, and multiplicity of special districts are among the top four problems on both lists. Streets and roads, tax base,

tax rates, sewage disposal and drainage, industrial development, continuing community leadership, community spirit, and
schools are among the top 15 on both lists. There is only one
marked shift in the rank ordering of the problems: freeways
and arterials moved up from twentieth place in Table 2 to a
second-place tie in Table 4.

The authors noted several differences among the classes of
leaders in their responses to the prepared list of problems. The
pro-annexation group in Hagginwood-Del Paso Heights and
the X group saw a greater number of area-wide problems, but
the general community leaders and the anti-annexation group
in Hagginwood-Del Paso Heights saw fewer. In fact, the most
clear-cut difference between a pro- and anti-annexation group
is seen in the two groups involved in the Hagginwood-Del
Paso Heights annexation attempt. Most problems the pro-
annexation group favors as most important, the anti-annexation
group sees as less important. The pro- and anti-annexation
groups in Arden-Arcade show more agreement, differing
mainly over multiplicity of special districts and mass transportation, which the pro-annexation group regards as more important. Both the general community leaders and the X group
emphasize freeways and arterials and redevelopment.

There are some inconsistencies between the responses of the
different classes of leaders to a request for personal description
of community problems and to the prepared list of problems.
For instance, the anti-annexation leaders in Hagginwood-Del
Paso Heights indicated more concern with long-range area-
wide planning in their personal evaluation, but less on the
prepared list of problems. These inconsistencies weaken the
characterizations of the particular movement involved, but
since different methods were used in obtaining the data, the
results do not have identical meaning even when the results
are consistent. As mentioned earlier, a leader may not think of

a particular problem when asked to describe what he considers to be area problems, but he may give the same problem a very high rating when it is brought to his attention. Also, because of the small number of problems mentioned by individual interviewees in response to the first question (Table 2), these results are probably more subject to sampling fluctuations than the results obtained from grading a list of problems. In other words, if leaders were asked to answer both questions a second time, the differences between the two answers to the first question would probably be greater than those between answers to the second question. The results from the second question (the list of problems) should probably be given more weight for that reason.

LEADERS' MEMBERSHIP AND REFERENCE GROUPS

Since community organizations often strongly affect a person's attitudes and behavior, the Sacramento leaders were asked about the relative influence of various groups and organizations in the county. When asked which groups would be effective in securing voter approval of some county-wide referendum, the leaders most consistently ranked the *Sacramento Bee* as the organization of greatest influence in the county. Elected and appointed officials of the county and the city, the chambers of commerce, and other news media are also seen as important. In all, 13 groups received mean ratings equivalent to "fairly important" or higher. Veteran, religious, political, and ethnic and racial groups are not so important, and senior military officers at local military installations received the lowest rating (see Table 5).

SMAAC-MGC leaders see political influence resting in the business community, news media, and city officials and discount the influence of political parties. The pro-incorporation leaders see political influence in much the same way as the group of lead-

TABLE 5

Leaders' Views of Influential Groups in Community

Organization	Mean Rating*
Sacramento Bee	3.8
Elected and appointed officials of Sacramento County	3.6
Chambers of commerce	3.5
Sacramento Union	3.5
Elected and appointed officials of the city of Sacramento	3.5
Television and radio	3.5
Neighborhood newspapers, such as the *San Juan Record,* or the *Suburban News-Shopper*	3.3
Large manufacturing companies, such as Campbell Soup Company or Aerojet-General Corporation	3.3
Government employee associations (city, county, and state)	3.2
Nonpartisan groups, such as the League of Women Voters	3.2
Labor unions, such as AFL-CIO	3.2
Professional societies, such as the County Bar Association or the County Medical Society	3.1
Large commercial enterprises such as Breuner's or Sears	3.0
Service organizations such as Rotary or Kiwanis	2.9
Smaller manufacturing or commercial companies	2.7
Veterans organizations such as the American Legion or VFW	2.5
Catholic religious groups	2.4
Protestant religious groups	2.4
Local Republican Party	2.3
Local Democratic Party	2.3
Jewish religious groups	2.3
Ethnic and racial groups such as the NAACP or the Japanese American Citizens League	2.2
Senior officers at local military installations	2.0

* Mean of ratings assigned where 4 equals very important; 3, fairly important; 2, not so important; and 1, not at all important.

ers as a whole. The pro- and anti-annexation groups in Hagginwood exhibit some sharp contrasts once again, especially in their views of the influence of the League of Women Voters,

ethnic and racial groups, and city officials, all of whom are seen
as more influential by the pro-annexation group. They agree,
however, that trade associations, neighborhood newspapers,
and religious groups are less influential, although leaders generally found them more important. Pro-annexation groups in
both Hagginwood and Arden-Arcade see the League of Women
Voters as more influential than the average leader does. The
anti-annexation leaders in Arden-Arcade tend to discount the
influence of several organizations that the leaders as a whole
regard as quite powerful. The general community leaders,
some of whom are executives of large commercial enterprises,
see such businesses as more influential than the average leader
does. Political parties were judged by the X group to have very
little influence on county issues.

In another question, the leaders were asked to say which
organizations helped them make up their minds on issues.
Again the *Bee* is seen as the most influential organization. Six
other sources are given as more than moderately helpful: business associates, city officials, county officials, personal friends,
the Sacramento City-County Chamber of Commerce, and the
Sacramento Union. Service clubs seem to be of little help in
this respect.

The leaders themselves are, of course, members of organizations (Table 6). Two-thirds or more of them are members of
welfare organizations such as United Crusade or American Red
Cross and of the YMCA and other youth groups, while only one-
third or fewer are members of employee groups, business associations, and veterans' groups. In view of the relatively low
social service interests of the general community leaders, we
may assume that their participation in welfare organizations
stems from religious or economic interests rather than social
service interests. Leaders from the suburban areas are relatively
less active in welfare organizations.

TABLE 6

Leaders' Participation in Community Organizations

Organizations (Arranged in order of over-all degree of participation)	SMAAC and MGC	New city incorporation (Pro)	Hagginwood Pro	Hagginwood Anti	Arden-Arcade Pro	Arden-Arcade Anti	General community leaders	X Group	Over-all
Welfare organizations	88%	69%	50%	67%	55%	44%	100%	87%	73%
Youth groups	55	81	50	33	77	55	88	87	69
Chambers of commerce	67	62	25	50	67	33	75	100	63
School organizations	55	87	50	67	44	44	58	50	63
Improvement clubs	44	56	100	50	100	77	50	25	62
Religious organizations	66	56	50	33	11	44	88	62	52
Professional organizations	66	44	0	33	66	55	33	87	49
Republican Party	44	69	100	33	22	66	58	62	46
Civic organizations	66	50	25	33	55	22	42	50	45
Service clubs	67	44	25	50	11	11	67	67	42
Labor unions and employee groups	55	25	50	0	55	44	12	25	33
Veterans' groups	22	31	0	33	22	22	16	50	26
Business associations	22	25	25	16	11	22	58	12	25
Democratic Party	33	31	0	16	11	0	0	37	18

Most of the X group, general community leaders, SMAAC-MGC, pro-annexation in Arden-Arcade, and pro-incorporation leaders belong to a chamber of commerce, and several are active in them. One-third or fewer of the pro-annexation group in Hagginwood and the anti-annexation leaders in Arden-Arcade belong to, or are active in, the chambers. A large proportion of the pro-incorporation leaders are active in school organizations while a relatively small proportion of the Arden-Arcade leaders on both sides have participated in such organizations.

A fairly striking difference among the movements occurs with respect to membership in improvement clubs. One hundred per cent of both pro-annexation groups were at least moderately active in improvement clubs. Less than half of the X group and SMAAC-MGC leaders belong to such organizations. A major objective of most improvement clubs is an increase in number of and an improvement in quality of the municipal services rendered. To the extent that the claim is accepted that annexation is the most effective means of achieving this, annexation becomes important to the club members. Membership in improvement clubs is more common in suburban neighborhoods than within the city, where many of the X group, SMAAC-MGC members, and general community leaders reside.

Forty-six per cent of the leaders report membership or activity in the Republican Party. The pro-annexation group in Hagginwood is made up entirely of Republicans; on the other hand, only 22 per cent of the Arden-Arcade pro-annexation group are Republicans, while 66 per cent of the Arden-Arcade anti-annexation group are Democrats. Over-all, only a small proportion (18 per cent) of the leaders studied is Democratic in a county that normally votes Democratic. Most of the leaders in the present study are employed in professional and managerial occupations—occupational groups which are more likely to be Republican than Democratic. However, there is no reason for believing that the leaders—whether Republican or Democrat—participated in the governmental reorganization struggles for partisan reasons.

Somewhat less than half of the leaders belonged to civic organizations. The variation from movement to movement in membership in civic organizations was smaller than for most other types of organizations listed in Table 6. Such membership is most characteristic of the SMAAC-MGC leaders.

MOTIVES FOR SUPPORTING REORGANIZATION

We wanted to learn what reasons leaders thought led to people joining one of the reorganization movements. As part of the personal interview, the leaders were asked to consider

TABLE 7

Motives for Joining Reorganization Movements
As Seen by 96 Leaders

Motive	Per cent*
Desire for more and better governmental services	63
A strong, continuing interest in achieving the most effective form of local government	59
Desire for lower taxes	45
Ownership of land or property which would be affected by reorganization	32
Occupation affected by reorganization	29
Desire for status and prestige	26
Desire for power and influence that could be exerted	23
Protection of a business which would be affected by reorganization	23
Attraction for opportunities for social interaction that the movement provided	22
A stepping stone to political office	18

* Percentage reported is the mean percentage given under the "very important" category.

those persons they knew who were active in one or more of the movements and, from a list of possible reasons, to give the proportion for whom they felt each was an important motivation. Table 7 shows that the first five reasons given by the 96 leaders for participation in the reorganization movements included desire for more and better governmental services, a continuing interest in achieving a more effective form of local government, desire for lower taxes, concern over property values, and concern over job security. Only a small proportion of activists, in the opinion of the interviewees, joined the movements as a means of gaining political office.

LEADERS' EXPECTATIONS FOR METROPOLITAN GOVERNMENT

All interviewees were asked to give their preference from a list of alternatives for metropolitan government reorganization (Table 8). They were then asked which alternative they felt

TABLE 8

The Future of Governmental Reorganization
In Sacramento—The Leaders' Views

Reorganization Plan	Preference	Expectation
	Per Cent	
City-county merger	40	5
Large-scale annexation combined with consolidation of as many city-county functions as possible (MGC report)	18	20
City-county merger excluding rural area (PAS without the rural)	11	10
One large incorporation of the North Area and additional annexation to existing cities	10	2
Large-scale annexation to city of Sacramento	7	19
Other*	10	19
Status quo	4	25

* No suggestions were made to interviewees as to what "other" might include, but interviewees may have had in mind changes such as several small incorporations.

was likely to be put into effect in the next three to five years. The alternative preferred by most people (city-county merger) is felt to be among the ones least likely to be in effect in the near future and the least preferred alternative (the *status quo*) is felt to be the most likely to continue to exist. A substantial proportion of the leaders feel that large-scale annexation with integration of many city-county functions (MGC report) is both desirable and likely to be adopted. This opinion supports those who see large-scale annexation to the city of Sacramento as a probable solution.

EVALUATIONS AND CONCLUSIONS

There is little agreement among selected judges in identifying the key leaders of the area. Only 28 persons were nominated by three or more of 18 judges, only one by as many as eight. Certainly, in this light Sacramento does not have the kind of power elite that Floyd Hunter found in Regional City (Atlanta). Some interviewees felt that the concentration of power in Sacramento had decreased with the rapid population growth since World War II and the decline of local ownership of businesses. Leaders named by three or more judges come predominately from the business community in the city of Sacramento. They were not active in the reorganization movements. They are satisfied with city and county government and although many prefer merger or large-scale annexation they do not regard governmental reorganization as an urgent necessity. Traffic and parking problems seem more important. They are aware of the conflicting opinions over proposed changes and some wish to avoid taking a stand on controversial matters. Although the state government is a major employer in the area, state officials were not named as key leaders.

With the single exception of the publishers of the *Sacramento Bee,* the most influential Sacramento leaders did not initiate any of the reorganization movements. Only nine of Sacramento's 28 most influential leaders (nominated by three or more judges) were known to have been active in any of the movements. Several of these were elected or appointed public officials who participated by virtue of their official positions. The movement leaders were not well known throughout the metropolitan area. They were drawn from the upper middle class, and while professionally able and well educated, they had only moderate community-wide influence.

The three most important problems facing Sacramento chosen by the leaders—long-range area-wide planning, consolidation of governmental services, and multiplicity of special districts—reflect their own strong theoretical bent but are unlikely to find as ready acceptance among the voters at large. There was less, though still substantial, agreement among the leaders interviewed on the importance of streets and roads, tax base, tax rates, sewage disposal and drainage, industrial development, continuing community leadership, community spirit, and schools. Except for the streets and schools, these issues probably do not deeply concern the average voter.

In the areas concerned in the annexation and incorporation proposals, a high proportion of home owners paid their taxes along with monthly mortgage payments in one lump sum. As long as the monthly payments seem reasonable, many taxpayers do not worry about taxes. They may be aware that several homes in the area have septic tanks, but as long as their own plumbing works they are not greatly concerned.

Many citizens fail to see a relationship between industrial development and their personal welfare. They have little direct knowledge of industrial development efforts. Often they assume that such efforts will bring additional "industrial" sections to the community. Such views may be particularly common among Sacramento's high proportion of government workers.

There seems to be little support for the notion that Sacramento leaders, much less Sacramento voter-citizens, recognized a common set of community-wide problems requiring new governmental forms for adequate solution. To be sure, several leaders saw urgent problems within the metropolitan area, but they had difficulty winning community-wide support for doing something about them. The general community leaders were concerned with traffic and parking, but naturally this did not seem a pressing problem to the suburban leaders. The multiplicity of special districts that seemed such a critical problem to the pro-annexation leaders seemed much less important to the general community and the anti-annexation leaders. While there were differences among leaders in different movements, there were also large variations within movements. Our data do not support the notion of a highly homogeneous group of leaders joining together to form a metropolitan government movement.

The failure of several attempts to change the governmental structure in the Sacramento metropolitan area may be partially explained by the lack of agreement among the politically influential organizations. The *Bee* has vigorously supported smaac, mgc, and the annexation proposals, and vigorously opposed the proposal to incorporate a new city. County officials have tended to support the *status quo*. Until recently, city officials have not vigorously supported annexation. When they have, as in the Arden-Arcade attempt, there is reason to believe that they have been opposed by at least some county officials. The Sacramento City-County Chamber of Commerce has taken official positions on several proposals but has not forcefully supported them. The *Union* has been much less concerned than the *Bee* with metropolitan governmental problems.

While there was substantial agreement among all leaders in identifying the most influential organizations, there were some meaningful differences among movements. Pro-annexation leaders tended to see city officials as politically more influential and personally helpful than anti-annexation and pro-incorporation leaders. The pro-incorporation leaders found suburban newspapers, which tended to support the movement, more helpful, and downtown newspapers, which opposed the movement, less helpful than did the average group. The general community leaders, some of whom were executives of large commercial enterprises, saw such organizations as more influential than did the average leader. Leaders tended to see area-wide political influence residing in those organizations which they personally found helpful in deciding about political issues and in organizations that supported their particular movement. This attitude is another reflection of the lack of organizations as well as individuals that are widely acknowledged as influential forces in the community.

The bulk of our interview and questionnaire data suggests that a conscious desire to obtain more and better governmental services through a more effective form of local government was the most important surface inducement for action. For the most part, those who sought change were public spirited citizens dissatisfied with the level and efficiency of governmental services. Those who opposed change were somewhat more likely to be concerned with possible tax increases, but they were also likely to feel that the proposed change was a poor means to a desirable goal.

It seems clear that once a person has taken part in one such movement he is more likely to participate in a second one. There is clear continuity of concern on the part of the most active leaders. Originally they were asked to participate by a friend or an acquaintance. Frequently they became acquainted in the first place through participation in fund-raising drives, youth groups, or neighborhood improvement clubs.

Only a few activists were motivated by immediate economic vested interests. A small but active minority clearly was motivated by threats to jobs or positions. Noncity firemen, sheriffs' deputies, school administrators, and special district employees played important though usually supporting roles. There were probably cases where participation was motivated by anticipation of a new job or position as well as by a threat to one presently held, but this seemed to be much less common. This probably is related to the relative uncertainty of job reward and the relative certainty of job threat.

Also, there is evidence that proposed changes directly affecting property values lead to activity on the part of the property owner. For example, the Arden Fair property owners were concerned with the possible extension of the city transit lines to their shopping area in the event the Arden-Arcade annexation passed.

If we accept the modern view that leadership is a relationship involving the characteristics of the leader; the attitudes, needs, and other personal characteristics of the followers; and the social, economic, and political situation in which the movement takes place, we can begin to see why none of the reform movements succeeded.[4] The movement leaders lacked community-wide influence and did not have the resources to carry out a sustained campaign. Sacramento does not have a power elite that is able to dominate metropolitan governmental decisions. The followers (the voters) are not greatly concerned with metropolitan governmental problems. The most serious problems lie in the future and are not yet readily apparent. The issues are complex and require careful study, which the average voter is unwilling to give.

No group now has the legitimate status and the necessary resources to study problems of the entire metropolitan area.

The functions of the city and county governments overlap and the personal interests of the officials do not always encourage them to take a broad community-wide view. In addition, state laws and constitutional provisions make city-county merger difficult to achieve. As a consequence, the citizens resort to the two remaining options—annexation and the establishment of special districts—when a problem becomes acute. Such changes, taking place at regular intervals during the past several years, have resulted in a reasonably adequate level of metropolitan services administered by a complicated and illogical system of overlapping jurisdictions.

7

Government in the Sacramento Area: Retrospect and Prospect

In the Sacramento area, what metropolitan-wide organizations are available for reorganization action? What are the shape and content of the leadership structure in the area? What alternative approaches are available to metropolitan Sacramentans when considering governmental change? Is there any common awareness, or sense of community, that extends throughout the Sacramento metropolitan area? These and related questions are explored further in this chapter, based largely upon the data, observations, and conclusions of previous chapters.

THE SACRAMENTO COMMUNITY

On the surface, it appears that governmental change should have a greater chance of success in Sacramento than in many other metropolitan areas in the United States. Sacramento has relatively few separately incorporated municipalities—only four since the merger of Sacramento and North Sacramento— with their resident loyalties and vested interests in preserving the *status quo*. Metropolitan Sacramento also is young, and therefore has not had decade after decade of building up encrusted governmental traditions. Still another reason is that professionalism, the professional frame of mind so congenial to reform, is a dominant aspect of the milieu. Yet, the final impetus to governmental integration, a sense of community, seems to be lacking.

"Community," of course, is a word of many meanings. Sociologists have speculated at length on the status of "community" in the Western world and some have deplored what they call the loss of community. Out of the considerable writings on the subject, however, one can extract an appropriate definition of community, which will serve as a guide in determining presence or absence of community in the Sacramento area. The bond that brings a group of people into a community is a set of commonly held beliefs regarding activities that presumably contribute to the general welfare of all. These beliefs may be political, social, cultural, religious, or economic, but they must be held widely enough to create a feeling of group identity, purpose, and destiny—a sense of community.

It is clear from the preceding chapters that in postwar Sacramento County there is little agreement on the best form of government or even on the need for some different form of government for the area. Even under the very doubtful assumption that state legal obstacles to city-county merger can be surmounted, the incorporated communities, including the city of Sacramento, would be unlikely to give up their identities.[1] No plan like that of Dade County in Florida, which would create some super-metro agency while leaving existing cities intact, has been proposed.

THE BONDS OF COMMUNITY IN SACRAMENTO

Superficially at least, characteristics other than geography and traditional loyalties seem to provide a potential agent for building greater community cohesion. There are social, cultural, religious, and economic ties within the metropolitan area. The city of Sacramento remains the primary cultural and social center for the entire area. Suburbanites as well as city-dwellers take advantage of its art galleries; its theater groups; its symphony orchestra; its summer music circus; its civic auditorium; its stadium, which is connected with the city unified school district; and its zoo. Very few such facilities are available elsewhere in the county. Traveling road shows, operas, lectures, art shows, and musical events come to the city of Sacramento if they come to the urban area at all. In addition, some suburban citizens often commute considerable distances to the city's churches, parks, and movie houses. A great deal of communication among the many subcommunities in the county comes through the use of churches, colleges, and recreational facilities.

But these cultural and social ties to the city are not sufficient to create a feeling of community. Whether they can become so is questionable. At best the attachment is a loose one and represents that of only a limited segment of the county population. Even this segment is as likely to turn to the San Francisco Bay area, 90 miles away, for entertainment and cultural advantages. Further, an almost endless variety of recreational opportunities at lakes, mountains, and the seashore is readily available outside the metro area.

In some communities one religion predominates and unites,

but in the Sacramento area, as in most communities, no one of the many denominations and sects embraces a majority of the population. Catholics are the largest single group. A recent poll indicated that more than 50 per cent of the people in the area belonged to no church.

Some nascent stirrings of common interest appear in the economic sphere. Of a county working population of 195,000, as of January 1, 1961, there were 60,000 government employees, one for every two and one-quarter persons employed in non-governmental work. Aerojet-General Corporation, which employs an additional 15,000 (this total has been decreasing in 1965 because of a reduced volume of federal government contracts), is wholly dependent on federal government contracts. If, in addition to this, we consider all of the jobs in the county which are supported by governmental activity (construction, supplies, equipment, services, food service, transportation, and so on), it is clear that metropolitan Sacramento is predominantly a government-subsidized area. Families who are supported by government and government-related enterprises are scattered widely throughout the whole area, and they may have many common ideas regarding the kind of community that would best serve them. Whether they can be welded into an active force giving the community a conscious sense of direction is an open question.

At present this large group is not agreed on the political organization of the community. Likewise there seem to be few commonly held views regarding the economic destiny of the area. This disparity could be expected. There is little need for close communication and coordination among most governmental agencies in carrying out their assignments. Employees are often highly specialized technical and professional workers who may share certain values with others in their field but these are not necessarily values relating to local government, services, and ways of life. The division among them over the desirability of attracting new industry to the metro area is typical. Some government employees feel that a great deal of industry will change the character of the population and would interfere with the existing basically sound and secure government-based economy. On the other hand, some government employees and other citizens agree with the business view that industry would widen markets and provide a broader tax base. This division of opinion has strengthened the primary forces that have barred new industry from locating in the metropolitan area.

Whatever the potential, even among government employees a "community" spirit does not now exist in Sacramento. The PAS found that,

> Evident in every aspect of life in the area is the fact that the county of Sacramento is one community. It has a common history, common social and economic interests, similar political characteristics, and a similar set of long-range goals. The people of the area pride themselves on being "Sacramentans," not because they live in a county with this name, but because they are proud of an historic capital city that has carried forward in the twentieth century the spirit and quality that marked the latter part of the nineteenth.[2]

No evidence was given to support this bold assertion. Merely stating that "Sacramento is one community" does not make it so, and the fate of the PAS proposal is certainly evidence to the contrary. Our interviewees repeatedly called attention to the antagonism between the people in the North Area and those of the city of Sacramento. Smaller cities emphasized their desire to be left out of any large-scale governmental reorganization. Citizens in Sacramento feared higher taxes would follow large-scale annexation. Almost without exception our interviewees deplored the apathy and lack of interest toward metropolitan area problems, but this atmosphere was accepted as unchangeable.

Sacramento County then cannot confidently be called a community, even though, by census definition, it may be a metropolitan area. The latter, an arbitrary statistical definition, has nothing to do with the final determinants of community action—the attitudes, beliefs, and motivations of real people. Creation of a "community" rests on the ability to gain acceptance of certain common goals or aspirations as desirable. Ultimately the recognition of serious, area-wide problems might create bonds of community that would lead to such acceptance of goals.

A SEARCH FOR MEANINGFUL PROBLEMS

The population of metropolitan Sacramento has almost doubled in ten years. But no one problem or group of problems seems to be serious enough or urgent enough to provoke general discussion among the citizens. This is evident from the results of the interviews, in which not even one-third of a representative group of leaders and residents could agree on important problems common to the area. The most common problems spontaneously offered by leaders and residents were the multiplicity of special districts and the need for long-range area-wide planning, but these were selected by less than 30 per cent of those asked. The need for governmental reorganization and the need for consolidation of governmental services were mentioned by 20 per cent and 16 per cent of the interviewees respectively.

Are these truly common problems? Are they meaningful to the voter-citizen, who must ultimately give consent to new governmental forms designed to solve them? "Fractionated government," a poor term at best, is no more of a problem to the resident of the city of Sacramento than is west-end development of the city to the resident of the North Area. To be sure, both of these are the problems of someone in the metropolitan area, but so far, pleas that these be considered as community-wide problems have fallen on deaf ears.

Some of our interviewees blamed the rejection of SMAAC-MGC proposals, as well as others, on the committees' failure to pinpoint actual problems, to give them a sense of urgency, to use pocketbook appeal. Converting problems into tax losses and gains is insufficient, however. Special districts are established because certain areas need particular services and the average citizen, who sees problems in concrete terms, is not impressed by the argument that elimination of those districts is in the interest of the entire community. Taxes and costs of government are important, but citizens must first agree on what their problems are before favorable community-wide action toward solutions—which, as a side effect, might result in cost savings—is obtained.

Most of the leaders of reorganization movements insisted that problems were real enough but that the public was apathetic. While this may be a rationalization for their failure, the assertion is true in the sense that citizens are apathetic because they do not sense a need for change. As we have seen, some citizens—namely, those in the Arden-Arcade area—had opportunities to incorporate as a part of the large new city and to annex to Sacramento. A few of them have considered incorporation as a separate small community. To date, each of these attempts has ended in failure. The alternatives, which have been proposed and not yet brought to vote, afford little hope for success. City-county merger (SMAAC report) has been mentioned often by citizens in the northeast area as the solution most favored, but the objectives of such a movement would probably appear no more immediate and desirable than those of other movements.

Two other reasons have been given by the leaders of reor-

ganization for the public apathy. The first, a common interpretation, is that most people already belong to so many social
and recreational groups and have so committed their time that
they have little left for local public affairs. The church organizations, PTA, boy and girl scouts, campfire girls, little leagues,
bowling leagues, boat clubs, ski clubs, neighborhood improvement clubs, bridge clubs, and tennis and swimming clubs have
more immediate importance to most heads of families than
participation in a movement to do something about metropolitan government. The general citizenry do not look ahead
but continue to vote for the *status quo,* confident that the
future will take care of itself somehow. The citizen feels help-
less to do anything about government anyway. It is too complex, too far removed from his immediate influence. One
interviewee cited, as an example of this attitude, the lack of any
complaint in the newspapers or to county officials when a
county road rapidly deteriorated soon after its completion.

Upon analysis, however, these two explanations of citizen
apathy lose much of their force. They do not explain why the
busy people who belong to many organizations did not give
money to the movements. In addition, if a situation is too complex for the ordinary citizen, he may support a group of leaders
who appear to understand the complexities, but the organizations described here did not win this trust. In short, satisfaction
with the *status quo,* not apathy, more accurately characterizes
prevailing attitudes. Unplanned growth has not been disastrous
in any material sense to the ordinary citizen; few obvious
severe problems have developed during the postwar years.

Some students of metro affairs would insist that area-wide
planning now would not only provide a much pleasanter way
of life but could prevent many of the incipient problems from
becoming serious. The jerry-built governmental service structures are sure to become severely strained as streets, sewers,

and water systems wear out and new housing tracts become slums. This may be, but this is prevention of future problems, not identification of immediate and severe problems. This type of trouble-shooting is wise but does not stir up the citizenry to join together in a united movement. For the time being, most metropolitan residents seem to believe that they are receiving adequate municipal-type services. The special district device provides avenues for those who want more or better services, and it avoids the uncertainties involved in major governmental reorganization.

The active county government probably makes annexation and incorporation, or even a total reorganization of the metropolitan governments, seem much less urgent or appealing. And the existing, although partially disguised, rivalry between the county and the city government presents an obstacle to the solution of area-wide problems, even if they were to be widely recognized.

VEHICLES OF COMMUNITY ORGANIZATION

If critical problems were to become manifest, what type of community organization could be made available for area-wide action? Where might the leadership that seems to have been absent in reorganization efforts thus far be found?

Certainly the voluntary organizations established for the purposes of achieving mass annexations and large incorporation have been unsuccessful in mobilizing community opinion and action. None of the voluntary groups was well organized for accomplishing the ends sought. While the original committee for incorporating the big North Area city did a good job of studying the problems for that area, the action organization was not effective. The only successful efforts during the two major annexation attempts were ones to obtain the signatures necessary to put the proposals on the ballot. Arden-Arcade people placed great reliance on informal contacts made through Democratic Party workers. But in both cases organizations for obtaining community approval were ineffective and consisted of but a handful of people. All of these organizations were *ad hoc,* because no existing organization had interests coterminous with the geographic area involved.

The effective opposition which defeated the Hagginwood-Del Paso Heights annexation, the large incorporation attempt, and the SMAAC and MGC plans was centered in one or more of the large, powerful, existing institutions in the area—namely, the city and county governments, the City-County Chamber of Commerce, the *Bee,* and in one case the school districts. Support by one of these institutions for a specific governmental change does not guarantee its success, but opposition from a major or even a minor institution appears to bring certain defeat to a proposal. Major institutions are already mobilized for action and have the advantage of being well financed, well organized, and having experienced leadership. The leaders of the incorporation movement stated that they were unable to respond to the opposition tactics of the *Bee* and city officials. They did not have access to communications media, and they lacked positions of authority and influence. The opponents of incorporation, without really organizing, reached the people by crying "higher taxes," "protect our schools," "city domination," "double taxation," and so on.

The *ad hoc* citizens' groups that were formed to oppose each movement were led by people with roughly the same leadership prestige, experience, and capabilities as those possessed by the supporters. The opposition to the Arden-Arcade annexation probably had more money at its disposal than the supporters, but this was not true of those opposing large-scale incorporation. Unquestionably, those opposing the Hagginwood-Del

Paso Heights annexation had at their disposal more money and other resources than did the proponents. Emphasis on single, simple issues was the outstanding characteristic of the opposition—in both the major community institutions and the citizens groups. Their opposition was essentially negative; they did not need to make alternative proposals.

While there are no effective organizations for achieving specific governmental changes, are there any for studying and proposing action on metropolitan area problems? The Sacramento Area Planning Association, a volunteer group established in 1953, was composed of a small number of citizens who were challenged by a problem this study found most seriously regarded—the need for long-range area-wide planning. The association never became well known in the community, did not agree on concrete problems, and never attempted to take area-wide action. The Urban Government Committee may have been established under stimulation from sapa, and the *Bee* studies and articles on governmental deficiencies in the unincorporated North Area may also have grown out of its work, but we found no evidence to support this interpretation. The association, which was disbanded in early 1960, was deterred from effective action primarily because its membership was not geographically or occupationally representative of the metropolitan area.

The *Sacramento Bee,* the area's largest and most powerful newspaper, was the first organization to study the unincorporated fringe around the city of Sacramento and to analyze the problems of the mushrooming suburban growth, and its work led directly to the creation of the Sacramento Metropolitan Area Advisory Committee. The paper specifically suggested that a commission be appointed to study the "crisis" that these articles had revealed. The Urban Government Committee of the Greater North Area Chamber of Commerce was also studying the problem—primarily from the viewpoint of the North Area—at the time of the *Bee* articles, but the public was not aware of its work, nor were local government officials influenced by it. Neither the Greater North Area Chamber of Commerce nor its Urban Government Committee is in existence today.

The SMAAC membership consisted entirely of persons selected by the governments in the county. SMAAC employed outside staff (Public Administration Service) to conduct the study, and SMAAC members did not participate in it. The subsequent report proposed a form of government virtually impossible to achieve because of constitutional provisions and its political unacceptability to sponsoring governments.

The Metropolitan Government Committee, which followed the demise of SMAAC, was appointed by essentially the same governmental bodies. By proposing mass annexation and recommending consolidation of certain functions, the report of MGC favored both the city and the county. Mass annexation has not taken place, however, and functional consolidation is still in the discussion stage. SMAAC and MGC recommendations have not found vigorous support from citizen groups or agencies backed up by widespread public support. Except for the *Bee*'s success in getting SMAAC started, all of these attempts to identify the area-wide problems and to mobilize public opinion and action have failed.

Sacramento, like many other communities, is overorganized. It has a plethora of professional and technical organizations with interests focused on specialized matters. Various health and welfare fund-raising organizations, California State Employees Association, United Crusade, service clubs, school boards, parent-teacher associations, and the legal, medical, and innumerable other professional associations all have active support. These competing specialized organizations impede creation and continuance of organizations with general metropolitan interests. There is also conflict and jealousy between the city of Sacramento and the giant, unorganized North Area and, paralleling this, rivalry between the city and the county. These opposing forces are probably the most serious impediment of all, because the proposal for one big city, which the powerful *Bee* and the City-County Chamber of Commerce have favored from the beginning, cannot even be studied objectively in a mutually competitive atmosphere. The representatives of these rival factions would come to an area-wide study and action group with biases and preconceived ideas of how their faction ought to fare.

Our interviewees' assertion that the *Bee* "pushed," "forced," or otherwise caused the city and county governments to act is significant. No comparable vehicle existed for initiating study of these problems, calling them to the attention of the people, and getting action under way. The newspaper was successful once, but the results of the action it inspired suggest that it did not truly represent community sentiment and generally recognized need.

No governmental agency has over-all responsibility to look after the problems of the area, and no private organization has assumed this responsibility. Who should do it? The City-County Chamber of Commerce, the League of Women Voters, political parties, a federation of service clubs, a permanent research organization, a new watchdog civic organization, or some combination of all of these might succeed, but plainly none of these is now effective. The civic graveyard is being filled with the remains of organizations that failed in the task.

THE MISSING LEADERS

Two important conclusions emerging from this study are that the traditional sources of leadership which has prestige and authority now produce few leaders in the Sacramento area, and that, for government reorganization, the metropolitan area is devoid of recognized, effective area-wide leadership.

Traditionally the primary leaders for most community activity have been the captains of business, finance, and industry, but these people have, with rare exceptions, refrained from taking a public position on metropolitan and local governmental reorganization issues in Sacramento. Study of the rosters of governmental reform ventures underlines this fact. The American community is so constituted that only business leaders have sustained power. When these individuals do not assume their traditional role and responsibility, a vacuum in the leadership of the community is created.

Why have business leaders failed to take up community leadership tasks? A partial answer lies in the changing business environment in Sacramento. Today the number of important, locally-owned firms is decreasing. The ones that do exist have little influence in the suburbs, where business is dominated by the corporate chain store. The growth of the chain store reveals another impediment to effective community leadership by businessmen. The local manager of a chain store, usually but one of many employees who hold similar positions in the company, competes within the company for a more important position. His life and welfare are wrapped up in the company. He is the modern organization man—more often than not, a junior-level executive. His participation in noncontroversial local fund-raising or cultural organizations is encouraged by the parent company to demonstrate his concern with local affairs. But he is definitely and firmly discouraged from making public statements or acting in controversial matters that might alienate a client or customer. At one time the local owner of a company or bank would run for public office or speak out on political issues. Today a comparable man is a branch manager, who is insecure in his position, eager for advancement, and who will not actively participate in political affairs or encourage his subordinates to do so. Aerojet-General Corporation in the Sacramento suburbs is an unusual exception to this corporate policy. Aerojet encourages its employees to be active in politics at local, state, and national levels and invites campaign speeches and party fund drives on company time and property. However, without some drastic reshifting of values, most of the local managers for large corporations, whose potential for local leadership is high, are lost to governmental affairs.[3]

In the traditional community a few political or labor leaders frequently supplement the leadership by business. However, both the county and the city of Sacramento have council-manager governments, which, while administratively desirable, do not provide strong political leadership. The managers, organization men themselves, are employed to carry out policy, not to initiate programs. Their bosses—councilmen or supervisors—usually act as a body. With few exceptions, county supervisors have not lent their support to any basic changes in the existing community structure. They pledge support to what the people want. This of course they must do, but as political leaders they can and ought to identify issues, point directions, and educate—as well as represent—the public. The city council and county board also lack individual political leaders. The group action that has been taken has naturally been in the interest of the established governmental structures.

Local state legislators, who more than any other political officials have positions of prestige and influence, have refrained from taking public stands on issues of community organization. Their motivation is undoubtedly the same as that of the private companies—they do not wish to alienate constituents. When the contending factions in the county can agree, the legislators are willing to support a program in the legislature, but they carefully avoid involvement in divisive issues of community organization. Their judgment is politically sound and is supported by the local political parties and political clubs, which do not encourage state legislative candidates to take stands on local issues.

The noninvolvement of political party organizations also conforms to the desires of most of the persons who were active in governmental reorganization movements. With few exceptions, the leaders felt that partisan politics had no place in local affairs. All local elections in California are nonpartisan and the *Bee* has long opposed partisan politics at the local level. Regardless of the reasons for inaction by experienced politicians and the political parties, groups seeking to make basic changes in the governmental organization are seriously hampered by lack of support from this part of the metropolitan community.

Labor leadership in community affairs in the Sacramento area is also practically nonexistent. Organized labor is not as strong as in most communities of this size because so many are employed by the government. Both the labor unions and their leaders have exercised little local political power.

One final traditional source of leadership is lacking in the Sacramento area. Although many persons are well-to-do, Sacramento does not have families with great fortunes, families that might devote a great deal of time to community affairs. The average personal income in the county is high, but the great majority of Sacramentans work for a living. There is no aristocracy of wealth which feels responsible for the welfare of the community.

If the traditional sources of personal community leadership have dried up or are nonexistent, what about the availability of alternative sources? Most of the other potentially strong leaders either do not have a stake in the community or, for policy reasons, are barred from overt activity which may be controversial. The heads of the three major military installations by tradition and decree must stay out of politics. Other federal employees can operate only under the limitations of the Hatch Act, which usually has been strictly construed, although employees are still free to engage in nonpartisan local activities.

Nearly all of the elected heads of the executive branch of state government reside in the Sacramento area, yet these and other nontenure state officials do not play a local role. Their interests center on state affairs and their usually short tenure makes them transients in the immediate community. Local citizens tend to be critical rather than appreciative of a state official's comments on a purely community matter, and discourage even those few who might become active locally.

Under the state civil service act, a career employee has considerable freedom to engage in political activity. But the kind of leadership needed in the community apparently is not nurtured in great governmental bureaucracies. Perhaps the upper-level career employees are so imbued with the tradition of civil service neutrality that they simply refrain from controversial public activity. Some are conscious of the negative attitudes of their superiors toward political involvement. Although a few have run for office, no state employee in Sacramento has served on a city council or the county board of supervisors in the postwar period, and none has been elected to the state legislature or to national office. State employees offer a good potential, but experience indicates that governmental officials or employees are not a fruitful reservoir of talent for local government matters.

PRESENT LEADERSHIP

Without exception, the persons who have led annexation and incorporation movements come from intermediate positions of prestige and influence. Most are professionally able persons with educational qualifications well above those of the traditional leader. They are idealistic. They have often had some experience in improvement clubs, political clubs, park districts, or local chambers of commerce. A few were state and federal employees. No person active in favor of one of the reorganization attempts was previously well known over the entire metropolitan area of Sacramento County, or even within the area for which change was sought. No one of them would have been mentioned as a county leader—in politics, business, or governmental affairs.

As actors in the reorganization attempts, each of these men was able to command the personal loyalty of only a handful of supporters. Their immediate followers rarely attracted more than a few helpers in petition and fund-raising attempts. The primary support for both the Hagginwood-Del Paso Heights and the Arden-Arcade annexation attempts came from a few persons associated with improvement clubs. Yet few members in these clubs were active in support of a movement. The incorporation leaders were not closely associated with any established organization, and the chambers of commerce, to which some of them belonged and in which they had held official positions, failed to respond to their call. None of the leaders was able to stimulate the business community to participate. Only the public relations officer from one large shopping center, the assistant manager of another, and a junior executive of a corporation ever joined one of the movements (incorporation); their company owners took no official position.

The conclusion that Sacramento lacks community-wide leadership is supported by the interviews with leading citizens. Most of the citizen-judges chosen had trouble naming ten community-wide leaders. Some, while readily admitting difficulty in identifying current community leaders, could recall names of leaders of 25 years ago—that is, the city of Sacramento's past generation of leaders. These were the leaders of an era when most of Sacramento County's population resided within the city of Sacramento and there was no suburban problem. Only one man was named as many as eight times in the replies of 18 judges. He is the recently retired Sacramento city manager, whose influence and power extended little beyond the city boundaries and at most to less than half the metropolitan population. As a professional manager he could not be said to wield the kind of political power with which we are here concerned and he did not presume to provide active leadership on controversial public issues. His power was properly that of an administrator, not a community innovator.

To obtain a list of ten community leaders we found it necessary to include people who had been mentioned only four times by the judges. Most of the list was composed of city dwellers, none of whom could be considered area-wide leaders; some of these frankly admitted in interviews that they did not consider themselves area-wide leaders. At the same time, most of them were unable readily to identify others who they believed were recognized community leaders. The interviewees expressed the same dismaying conclusion expressed above—that the potential leaders are not vitally interested in metropolitan area problems, are engrossed in their own affairs, and see no urgency in the so-called "crisis of growth."

POTENTIAL LEADERSHIP

Numerically the greatest potential source for leadership, able to tackle the tough and intricate problems of metropolitan growth, is the public employees. At the California capital a substantial percentage of the employees are well educated, capable, experienced in dealing with complex affairs, and able to establish and lead large-scale organizations. Public employees, although few in number, were more in evidence than representatives from any other groups on both sides of the mass annexation and incorporation movements. They were not, however, top administrators. But, regardless of their qualifications, government employees are politically impotent. However brilliant, they have rarely attained the community-wide status of the successful businessman or banker. Practically all urban Americans hold in highest esteem those who are most able to utilize for private purposes the economic resources of the community. The public servant's leadership status is low. The taxpayer-citizen resents his claim on the public pocketbook and looks upon him as a servant, not a leader. In this environment the career employee abstains from overt political action. He may be concerned with political affairs, but circumstances prevent him from seeking an important role.

The obstacles to providing civic leadership from high level state government employees are obviously great. A new image of public servants would have to be created—perhaps through radio, television, and other news media. The business community would have to help to build the prestige of this potential for community leadership that they, the traditional leaders, have been reluctant to assume. The governor, legislators, and department heads would have to permit their top echelon of employees to participate in local affairs, even controversial ones. Even if these external obstacles were surmounted, there are such additional, more subtle, problems as conflicts of interest and maintenance of neutrality of civil servants. Finally, the public employee himself would have to be willing to take on local problems. Merely listing some of the major obstacles to a change in status and role of public employees indicates that the chances of such a change are slim indeed.

School administrators and teachers, women's organizations, and minority groups are also unlikely sources of strong community leadership. Professional men and women—doctors, law-

yers, clergy, college professors—have a prestige of sorts, but
most are like the businessman, too concerned with the private
world of "getting and spending," too afraid of damage to
reputations, or too busy with their personal affairs and professional organizations to lend their energies to community-wide
political activities.

AND WHAT OF THE FUTURE?

Metropolitan Sacramento has almost doubled in size in the
last ten years and promises to redouble in the next 15. Future
governmental changes are inevitable, and the rapid growth will
surely hasten them. Will the changes tend to follow the basic
pattern of the *status quo*—with minor incorporations here and
there—or will there be a break with the present trend and
development of substantial governmental consolidations, even
of major governmental integration for the entire metropolitan
area?

Some observers maintain that the present network of many
special park, water, lighting, sewer, and other districts provides
fairly adequate service and allows a greater number of citizens
to participate directly as managers and board members. The
voters may participate in and do exert real political influence
on the establishment of the districts. They continue to affect
policy through periodic elections of the boards. This personal
involvement is impossible under total metropolitan government
with its magnitude and complexities. Special districts and iden-
tifiable community entities broaden the base for democratic
participation and provide a more intimate relationship between the citizen and his government.

Critics of the *status quo* emphasize the wastefulness in this
arrangement and point to the wide variation in level of services.
Under the special district system there has been no broad,

long-range planning for the metropolitan area. They argue that "grass roots" democracy in district government is more illusion than reality. Certainly special districts, and to a limited extent separate cities, have been created without reference to any general plan for the total area. These developments are anathema to the well ordered mind and to those who see a need to plan and develop the resources of the total area for the common interest.

The benefits of truly metropolitan-wide planning have never been presented to the people, say some critics. The citizen knows what he has and seems fairly well satisfied in spite of the reorganizers' predictions of future problems in water, slums, crime, sewage, and streets. A more desirable physical and cultural way of urban life has never really been presented in concrete terms. The SMAAC-PAS report, emphasizing borough government and elimination of existing governmental structures, failed to go beyond the obvious problems of simplifying governmental structure or of providing some services more effectively. The average citizen is more inspired by an over-all plan for development of cultural centers, parks and open spaces, river-bank recreational facilities, and zoning regulations that insure more than the mere separation of residences from commerce and industry.

Another explanation for the failure of reorganization movements arises out of suggestions made during our interviews. While the officials and planners have studied desirable objectives for the community, the citizens have never participated in discussions of these objectives, nor have they been consulted on the results. The major studies of the area were done by government-sponsored agencies and by the newspaper staff, which prepared the articles on conditions in the unincorporated parts of the county. No study dealt with more than Sacramento

County, although parts of neighboring counties are clearly within the actual Sacramento metropolitan area.

These interviewees suggest establishing a "blue ribbon" committee made up of people of the highest prestige and respect, and broadly representative of community interests—business, labor, churches, parent-teacher associations, improvement clubs, service clubs. Thus, even if the members individually lacked community-wide prestige, all of the important interests of the community would be represented. The committee, which would be staffed to assure adequate research, communication, and publicity, would conduct a thorough inventory of the services and functions of the metropolitan area. It would function like a federal or state commission—that is, provide professional research supplemented by public hearings for fact-finding and determination of public attitudes. The results could then be compared with the best in other governmental systems—the best parks, the best water system, the best cultural facilities, the best health services, and so on. Superiorities as well as deficiencies in the Sacramento metropolitan area would become evident. The citizens' committee, in making positive recommendations, would have definite ideals in mind. The result of such a citizen effort might not conform to a planner's dream, but it would have the merit of providing standards against which the citizen could compare what he has now with what he wants and is willing to pay for.

Given the conditions found in Sacramento by this study, the prospect for any major change in the *status quo* is not bright. To date, at least, the people of the area do not think of themselves as a single community; no suitable community-wide organization for identifying issues and promoting action exists; there is rivalry between the city and the county, and between the city and the large North Area; area-wide leadership that could marshal cohesive sentiment around comprehensive metropolitan-wide objectives is lacking. In the meantime, since there are no obvious immediate problems in Sacramento, the general citizenry can hardly be blamed for seeming content with the *status quo*.

POSTSCRIPT

As of June 1, 1965, the Hagginwood-Del Paso Heights annexation (discussed in Chapter Four) has been virtually completed—not by one annexation as originally attempted but by a series of smaller annexations. These, plus numerous other annexations and the merger of North Sacramento with the major city, have increased the area of the city of Sacramento to 92.75 square miles. On January 1, 1961, the area was 50.25 square miles, as compared with 23.46 square miles on October 1, 1955, the approximate date of the *Bee*'s "crisis" articles. This growth can hardly be said to represent mass annexation as recommended by MGC, however.

Aside from the piecemeal but sizable growth of the city of Sacramento, reorganization of government in the metropolitan area has proceeded slowly. Agreement on consolidation of functions will result soon after 1965 when Sacramento County performs the property assessment and tax collection functions for all cities in the county and operates a new metropolitan airport as well as the former Sacramento Municipal Airport. The city of Sacramento seems destined to operate a consolidated city-county library. City and county prosecutor offices were consolidated in the county office. There have been inconclusive discussions regarding consolidating city and county animal pounds and the planning functions. The city-county consolidation proposal of SMAAC-PAS is rarely mentioned in the press. However, there is an obvious lessening of rivalry between city and county.

From time to time incorporation sentiment has sprung up in the heavily populated unincorporated suburbs. Residents of Carmichael, Rancho Cordova, Citrus Heights, Orangevale, and Fair Oaks have actively discussed incorporation. On the basis of these expressions of interest, the Metropolitan Development Committee of the Sacramento City-County Chamber of Commerce investigated the feasibility and economy of some proposed incorporations. The committee's report, issued in the summer of 1961, expressed serious reservations about the desirability of incorporation but urged the Sacramento city council and the county board of supervisors to reconsider MGC's proposals. The chamber report triggered the formation of a small voluntary committee of area businessmen associated with the chamber, called the Sacramento Citizens' Committee on Incorporation. This committee recommended that the city council annex a 115-square-mile area northeast of the city. The committee also suggested that the council select an "area-wide committee on better urban government." However, no specific request for annexation of this large area ever came before the Sacramento city council, and the area-wide committee has not materialized.

On June 2, 1964, the voters of the city of North Sacramento approved merger with the city of Sacramento by a narrow margin of 16 votes. This merger added 6.58 square miles and 13,219 people to the city of Sacramento, for a total population of 262,500. The merger was reported to be the first in California in a period of 28 years. A strong argument for the merger was that the city of Sacramento completely surrounded the smaller municipality.

One recent development may be of real significance for governmental reorganization—the establishment of the Sacramento Local Agency Formation Commission. This commission, and its authority, are new factors on the local governmental scene. A state statute, effective on September 20, 1963, provides that a local agency formation commission shall be established in every California county.[4] The law calls for a five-member commission consisting of two county officers appointed by the board of supervisors, two city officers and an alternate, and a public member. The city members and the alternate are appointed by a city selection committee of representatives of each city in the county, and the public member is appointed by the other regular members of the commission. The alternate serves whenever a proposal affecting the city of one of the regular city representatives is before the commission, the latter being disqualified. Sacramento County's Local Agency Formation Commission consists of two members of the county board of supervisors, the mayor of Sacramento, the mayor of Folsom, and a local lawyer. The alternate member is the mayor of Galt. The executive officer appointed by the commission is M. D. Tarshes, Sacramento County executive officer.

The commission's specific duty is to review and approve or disapprove proposals for the incorporation of cities, the creation of special districts, and the annexation of territory to existing cities and special districts. School districts are not included under this power. The more general charge to the commission is that it shall adopt standards and procedures for the evaluation of proposals for the creation of, and annexations to, cities and special districts. The statute stipulates certain factors that should be considered by the commission, including the number of people involved, assessed valuation of land, land area, topography, and drainage. The commission is also directed to study the need of the area for organized community services beyond those now being received, and the relationship of the proposal to mutual social and economic interests and to the local government structure of the county. The county board of supervisors is to furnish the commission with necessary supplies, equipment, and operating funds.

After the usual procedures of filing of documents of intentions and public hearings, the commission's decision on a reorganization proposal is final. This is the key to the commission's power. If the commission refuses to approve a proposal for governmental change, no action can be taken on it for at least one year. If the commission approves the proposal, the proceedings for annexation or incorporation follow in the usual manner.

It is too early to predict the influence of the commission on governmental organization. Its potential influence is limited by the fact that it cannot initiate proposals for change. The commission could, however, prevent the proliferation of special districts and small cities. Conceivably the commission's decisions could lead to further governmental integration in the metropolitan area. But, as with other organizations examined in this study, the commission can accomplish positive action only with the understanding and support of the citizens of the metropolitan area.

Appendix

RESEARCH METHODS

The study of the decision-making process in metropolitan affairs may be approached in two different ways. Both methods of approach were employed in this study. In one, the researchers seek to identify the individuals and organizations involved in particular decisions through case studies in depth. A well known and outstanding study of this type is *Politics, Planning, and the Public Interest,* in which Meyerson and Banfield examined a series of decisions on the location of public housing projects in Chicago.[1] Our surveys of the two efforts to study metropolitan problems in an organized manner and the three attempts to achieve specific governmental changes follow this general pattern.

In the other approach, the researcher attempts to identify the individuals with general influence in the community and to ascertain their attitudes and actions in relation to community issues. In the now classic study of this sort, *Community Power Structure,* Floyd Hunter sought to find the central decision makers for the entire community of Regional City (Atlanta).[2]

We were looking for the same group of persons in our investigation of the general community leadership in the Sacramento metropolitan area; our findings are presented in Chapter Six.

Three main sources of information were used for the depth studies (Chapters Two through Five): official records and documents, newspaper accounts, and personal interviews. The minutes of the meetings of SMAAC, MGC, and the Urban Government Committee of the Greater North Area Chamber of Commerce, the proponents of the big new city idea, and other groups were referred to extensively. Official reports were issued by Public Administration Service, SMAAC, MGC, and other groups and agencies, and these and other available official records and documents were collected and examined. This is true also of the propaganda literature issued by supporters and by opponents of specific proposals. Day-by-day clippings were made from the two daily newspapers and from the weekly suburban newspapers and shoppers' guides in Sacramento from the earliest stages of this research project on. We also made use of back issues of these newspapers.

The extensive personal interview program was the most important source of information for the depth studies. Three classes of persons were interviewed: those who had been closely identified with one or more of these movements; general community leaders—that is, persons who might be expected to be leaders in the community although they did not take part in the surveys and movements for change; and persons who had been involved in some manner with the study and action proposals without being closely identified with any particular one (referred to as the X group).

Having agreed upon the classes, we turned to the selection of the specific individuals to be interviewed. Eighteen "judges" were asked to name the ten "real leaders" in the metropolitan area and to list the most influential persons in the reorganization movements. (Chapter Six of this study gives details on the kinds of persons selected as "judges" and on their answers.) About one-third of the persons mentioned most frequently as the more powerful and influential people in the entire Sacramento area were known to have been active in a particular movement. The remaining two-thirds were placed in our general community leaders class, and 14 were interviewed.

We relied upon three sources for determining the activists in the movements: names given by the judges, names drawn from our own personal knowledge of the activities of various persons in the community, and names from a special card file of persons mentioned in newspaper accounts of governmental reform activities.

From 14 to 20 persons were interviewed from each of the attempted action programs and from SMAAC and MGC combined. In addition to our original 18 judges, 96 persons were interviewed. Table 3 in Chapter Six classifies the 96 interviewees as to the role in which they were interviewed. The response to requests for interviews was exceptionally good. Only three persons declined to cooperate. The interviews ran from two to four hours each.[3]

Several interview schedules were developed in order to provide a common structure for describing the movements and to assure a reasonable degree of uniformity. Interview Schedule A sought the views of all 96 interviewees on the local governmental picture in general, and their interest in and involvement with local government matters. All persons were also asked to judge the relative importance of several metropolitan area problems listed.

Persons closely connected with the specific study and action movements were asked questions from Interview Schedule B, which centered on the particular study or movement with which the interviewee had been involved. Who participated in the movement, what interests influenced the movement, how was it financed, what was right or wrong about it, and other similar questions were asked. The interviewees also were asked to grade a list of possible motives for becoming involved and a list of preferences for governmental arrangements in metropolitan Sacramento.

The general community leaders and the "X" group were asked about various efforts at change from a general and overall point of view (Interview Schedule C). These interviewees also were asked about the motives behind participation in these efforts and about their own desires for government in the Sacramento area.

Upon completion of each interview, a Leadership Questionnaire and a copy of the Allport-Vernon-Lindzey "Study of Values"[4] were left with the interviewee. He was asked to fill them in and return them to us with no personal identification in a prepared envelope. From a total of 96 interviewees, 75 per cent complied with this request. The Leadership Questionnaire sought detailed information about the interviewee's personal life—his occupation, family, religion, education, membership in organizations, and types of periodicals read.

As soon as possible after completing an interview the interviewer recorded (either by tape or by hand) the information and ideas obtained in the interview in considerable detail. The interviewer expanded the notes taken on the interview schedules during the course of the interview and these expanded notes were then transcribed on cards which served as a permanent record of the information, ideas, and allegations given in the interviews.

Initially we had planned that the sociologist in our team would provide a general survey of the demographic and sociological factors relevant to metropolitan Sacramento, along with specific items pertinent to each of the study and action movements under study by the political scientists. The economist was to prepare a similar analysis of economic characteristics. The psychologist was to conduct the study of community leadership. Later, when the minimum number of persons to be interviewed turned out to be so great, the economist and sociologist had to aid in conducting interviews and preparing a description and analysis of a particular action movement. Each interviewer conducted the study of a reorganization movement and wrote up his findings. Only the psychologist experienced the luxury of staying with his original assignment. Each member of the interdisciplinary research committee, however, carefully reviewed the completed study from the perspective of his own academic field.

Notes

Preface

1. For a more thorough discussion of the problems encountered in designing the research project, see Lyman A. Glenny, "The Problems of Project Design for the Study of Metro-Government Movements," *The Western Political Quarterly*, XII, No. 2 (June, 1959), 578.

Chapter 1

1. Allan Temko, "Sacramento's Second Gold Rush," *Architectural Forum* (October, 1960), 124.

2. *Ibid.*

3. The term "metropolitan area" in its common usage refers to a densely populated area of considerable size which socially and economically is one community, irrespective of governmental boundaries. Commonly, many separate local governments are contained within such an area. The U. S. Bureau of the Census defines a standard metropolitan area as a county or a group of contiguous counties containing at least one city of 50,000 inhabitants or more. Contiguous counties not having a 50,000 population city of their own are included only if they are essentially metropolitan in character and are socially and economically integrated with the large

city of the neighboring county. If any part of a county is considered part of a metropolitan area, then the entire county is so considered. U. S. Bureau of the Census, *Local Government In Standard Metropolitan Areas* (Washington, D. C.: U. S. Government Printing Office, 1957).

4. United States Census Reports.

5. "Legislators Cite Sacramento County in Report on Special Districts," *Sacramento Bee*, January 19, 1961.

6. Charter of the city of Sacramento, Art. III, Sec. 17.

7. State of California, Department of Employment, *Distribution of California's Civilian Employment by Major Industry and Area, 1946-1957*, Report 352A, No. 12 (November 25, 1958).

8. State of California, Department of Employment, *Community Labor Market Surveys—California, 1958* (unpaged).

9. Information on income supplied by Sacramento City-County Chamber of Commerce.

10. "North Area Sets 4 Way Fringe Study," *Sacramento Bee*, November 15, 1955.

11. *Problems of Local Government in the Greater North Area of Sacramento County*, an Interim Report of the Urban Government Study Committee of the Greater North Area Chamber of Commerce.

Chapter 2

1. The provision that SMAAC was to act in an advisory capacity to the governmental bodies later became the basis of argument as to whether the final report belonged to the survey agency employed by SMAAC, to SMAAC, to the city councils and the board of supervisors, or to the public.

2. The minutes for every meeting of SMAAC have been examined. Much of the information given in this chapter about the work and organization of SMAAC is based upon these minutes.

3. SMAAC minutes, March 6, 1956.

4. "Area Advisory Group, Caught in A Lull, Hunts A Job to Do," *Sacramento Union*, September 5, 1956.

5. "Metropolitan Area Study: First Interim Report," November 13, 1956.

6. "Metropolitan Area Study: Second Interim Report," February 19, 1957.

7. *The Government of Metropolitan Sacramento* (Public Administration Service, 1957), pp. 120-24.

8. SMAAC minutes, May 27, 1957.

9. "Amendment Is Called Key to Merger," *Sacramento Bee,* July 2, 1957.

10. Opinion of Edmund G. Brown, Attorney General; Paul M. Joseph, Deputy Attorney General. No. 57/140.

11. *Final Report by the Sacramento Metropolitan Area Advisory Committee on the Metropolitan Area Study,* September, 1957.

12. "Isleton Only County Chamber Opposed to Merger Proposal," October 18, 1957. The headline is misleading in that it conveys the idea that all others were in favor. Some had taken no stand.

13. "Solons Think Amendment to Permit City-County Merger is Long Way Off," *Sacramento Bee,* November 6, 1957.

14. Overheard by one of the authors of this study.

15. California Assembly Interim Committee on Municipal and County Government, *Transcript of Proceedings,* Sacramento, December 5, 1957.

16. "SMAAC Seeks Accord in Row with North City," *Sacramento Bee,* November 20, 1957.

17. "SMAAC Decides to Ask Sponsors for Extension," *Sacramento Bee,* December 3, 1957.

18. "City-County Favor New Merger Group," *Sacramento Union,* December 19, 1957; "Proposal for Merger Study Group Gets Okey," *Sacramento Bee,* December 19, 1957.

19. "Council Okehs Plan on New Area Group," *Sacramento Bee,* December 27, 1957.

20. "Cowan Says Small City Setup Will Weaken Metro Structure," *Sacramento Union,* January 10, 1958.

21. "SMAAC Has Last Meeting, End Nears," *Sacramento Bee,* January 14, 1958.

22. "Metropolitan Government Committee of 21 Organized," *Sacramento Bee,* February 20, 1958.

23. MGC minutes, March 12, 1958; "MGC Will Ask County-Cities' Planners Advice," *Sacramento Bee,* March 13, 1958.

24. "Interim Report Relating to Services and Costs of Municipal Government in the Northeast Area of Sacramento County, by Function and by Listed Services," typewritten and undated copy.

25. "Arden-Arcade Annex Backed by MGC Unit," *Sacramento*

Union, March 3, 1959. This annexation movement was begun December 18, 1958.

26. *Government Reorganization for Metropolitan Sacramento,* final report of the Metropolitan Government Committee, June, 1959.

27. "City Must Do Its Share to Justify Annexation," *Sacramento Bee,* August 20, 1959.

28. "Tarshes Weighs Possible Consolidation Methods for Area," *Sacramento Bee,* January 30, 1964.

Chapter 3

1. There is uncertainty as to the official name of the organization which sponsored the incorporation proposal. The file of minutes of all meetings from March 3 through June 20, 1958, is labeled "Citizens Committee for Incorporation." Until June 2, each set of minutes was labeled simply as Minutes of the Committee. The minutes for June 2, 9, and 18, and the "Planning for Tomorrow" pamphlet, used the title of "Interim Committee on Incorporation of Greater North-East Area."

2. Information based on 1960 United States census reports for 23 census tracts, which approximate the boundaries suggested for incorporation.

3. See Chapter Seven for analysis of this test.

4. "New City in North Area Is Prospect," *Sacramento Bee,* January 31, 1958.

5. *Carmichael Courier,* July 3, 1958.

6. "Northeast City of 150,000 Is Proposed," *Sacramento Bee,* June 18, 1958; "Move Launched to Form Big North Area City," *Sacramento Union,* June 18, 1958; "Incorporation of Large Area Seen As Only Answer to City Politicians," *Carmichael Westerner,* June 19, 1958.

7. "Move to Form City Is Traced to Inaction," *Sacramento Bee,* June 18, 1958.

8. "Northeast Group Spurns City Wooing," *Sacramento Bee,* June 20, 1958.

9. "Sacramento City Blasts Charges on Annexation," *Sacramento Bee,* June 23, 1958.

10. California state law requires the signatures of at least 25

per cent of the landowners owning at least 25 per cent of the total land value in the area proposed for incorporation.

11. "Exclusive Petition for New City Cannot Be Extended," *Sacramento Bee*, September 15, 1958.

12. "Second Petition for New City May Go to Court," *Sacramento Bee*, October 9, 1958.

13. "Chamber of Commerce Board Okehs Idea of Single Big City," *Sacramento Bee*, September 23, 1958.

Chapter 4

1. "Del Paso Heights Meeting Favors Annexation," *Sacramento Bee*, July 17, 1958.

2. "Suburban C of C Maps Fight to Form New City," *Sacramento Bee*, January 26, 1957.

3. Demographic material was computed from U. S. census data, 1960, for seven census tracts that closely approximate the annexation area.

4. "Annexation Papers Get City Okeh," *Sacramento Union*, July 25, 1958.

5. "Annex Signers Top 3000; Vote Seems Assured," *Sacramento Bee*, October 13, 1958.

6. "Annexation to Whom?" *North Sacramento Journal*, July 11, 1958.

7. "School Districts' Status in Annexation Plan is Sought," *Sacramento Bee*, September 18, 1958.

8. "Ruling Says City Can Annex or Bar Schools," *Sacramento Bee*, September 4, 1958.

9. "Annex Voting Will Be Set," *Sacramento Union*, November 16, 1958.

10. "North Area CC Directors Vote Against Annex," *Sacramento Bee*, November 21, 1958.

11. "Burkhard Says Annex Would Get Tax Benefits," *Sacramento Bee*, November 13, 1958.

12. Sacramento City Unified School District, November 24, 1958.

13. Sacramento City Unified School District, December 8, 1958; "Job Security Would Get Study in Annexation," *Sacramento Bee*, December 15, 1958.

14. Sacramento City Unified School District, January 8, 1959.

15. *A Study of the Proposed Annexation of the Hagginwood-Del Paso-Gardenland Area to the City of Sacramento and Its Effect on the Educational Program of the American River Junior College District*, December 15, 1958.

16. Robert Curry, "A Study of Tax Predictions Made During Annexation Election Campaigns in Sacramento County, 1958-1960," Master's thesis, Sacramento State College, Sacramento, California, December, 1960.

17. "North School Heads Call Annex Defeat Spur to Unifying," *Sacramento Bee*, January 21, 1959.

The 1959 session of the California State Legislature eased the pressure for unification by providing that political annexation to a city would not include school annexation without the consent of the school districts involved. This gave protection against carving up school districts, but it also removed the urgency for school districts to unify. The school districts in the annexation area have not unified.

18. "Azevedo Thinks Second Annex Vote Would Pass," *Sacramento Union*, January 22, 1959.

Since the failure of this large-scale annexation attempt, several smaller efforts in the same area have been successful. The entire area, except for McClellan Field, of this attempted large annexation now is a part of Sacramento city.

Chapter 5

1. All 1960 census material presented in this section was obtained from U. S. Census Bureau, "Advance Final Data from the 1960 Census" for Sacramento County.

2. "North Area Group Wants Area Study," *Sacramento Bee*, September 18, 1958.

3. "City Approves Arden-Arcade Annex Start," *Sacramento Bee*, February 6, 1959.

4. "Council Okehs Arden-Arcade Annex Sign-up," *Sacramento Bee*, April 3, 1959.

5. "Arden-Arcade Annex Signup Will Be Explained," *Sacramento Bee*, April 15, 1959.

6. "Arden-Arcade Annex Move Is Validated," *Sacramento Bee*, June 15, 1959.

7. "Annexation Foes List 4 Main Objections," *Sacramento Bee*, June 12, 1959.

8. "Arden-Arcade Annex Vote Is Assured," *Sacramento Bee*, August 14, 1959.

9. "Foe Says Taxes Would Rise with Annexation," *Sacramento Bee*, August 19, 1959.

10. "City's Annexation Policies Are Listed," *Suburban News-Shopper*, September 10, 1959.

11. "Annex, Says Northern CC," *Sacramento Union*, September 11, 1959.

12. From a carbon copy of the letter, dated October 5, 1959.

Chapter 6

1. See research methods in Appendix. See also, Floyd Hunter, *Community Power Structure* (Chapel Hill: University of North Carolina Press, 1953).

2. In addition to the questions asked of all interviewees, a special set of questions was prepared for this group. One of the nominees was very busy during the period in which the interviews were being made and it proved impossible to arrange a satisfactory time for the interview. A substitution was made by selecting a person in a comparable position.

3. Eduard Spranger, *Types of Men*, trans. by Paul J. W. Pigors (Halle: Max Niemeyer Verlag); Gordon W. Allport, Philip E. Vernon, and Gardner Lindzey, *Study of Values* (New York: Houghton-Mifflin Co., 1960).

Following is a brief characterization of Spranger's types: the dominant interest of the theoretical man is the discovery of truth; the economic man is characteristically interested in what is useful; the aesthetic man sees his highest value in form and harmony; the highest value for the social man is love of people; the political man is interested primarily in power, although his activities are not necessarily within the narrow field of politics—whatever his vocation, he reveals his concern with power; the highest value of the religious man may be called unity—he is mystical, and seeks to comprehend the cosmos as a whole, to relate himself to its embracing totality. Spranger does not imply that a given man belongs exclusively to one or another of these types of values. His depictions are entirely in terms of "ideal types." Most individuals have mixed interests.

4. See, for example: Cecil A. Gibb, "Leadership," in Gardner Lindzey, *Handbook of Social Psychology*, v. II (Reading, Mass.: Addison-Wesley Publishing Co., 1954) and Douglas McGregor, *The Human Side of Enterprise* (New York: McGraw-Hill Book Co., 1960), pp. 182-85.

Chapter 7

1. North Sacramento, however, has done so. See Postcript to this study.

2. *The Government of Metropolitan Sacramento* (Chicago: Public Administration Service, 1957), p. 36.

3. The U. S. Chamber of Commerce and the American Medical Association have recently urged greater political activity by their members. How successful these urgings will be remains to be assessed.

4. California, *Statutes of 1963*, c. 1808.

Appendix

1. Martin Meyerson and Edward C. Banfield, *Politics, Planning, and the Public Interest* (Glencoe, Ill.: The Free Press, 1955).

2. Floyd Hunter, *Community Power Structure* (Chapel Hill: University of North Carolina Press, 1953).

3. In our interviews we were not able, of course, to record every single word uttered by the interviewees. Thus the quoted comments in the study are not always literally precise, though the essence and nuances of comments are retained.

4. Gordon W. Allport, Philip E. Vernon, and Gardner Lindzey, *Study of Values* (New York: Houghton-Mifflin Co., 1960). See Chapter Six for results of this test.